A FULL LIFE IN A
SMALL PLACE

A Full Life in a Small Place
and other essays from a desert garden

JANICE EMILY BOWERS

The University of Arizona Press
Tucson & London

The University of Arizona Press
Copyright © 1993
Arizona Board of Regents
All Rights Reserved

♾ This book is printed on acid-free, archival-quality paper.
Manufactured in the United States of America

97 96 95 94 93   5 4 3 2

LIBRARY OF CONGRESS CATALOGING-IN-PUBLICATION DATA
Bowers, Janice Emily.
A full life in a small place : and other essays from a desert
garden / Janice Emily Bowers.
        p. cm.
    ISBN 0-8165-1345-7 (acid-free paper). —
    ISBN 0-8165-1357-0 (pbk. : acid-free paper)
  1. Gardening—Arizona.   2. Desert gardening—Arizona.
  3. Garden ecology—Arizona.   4. Desert ecology—Arizona.
  1. Title.
SB455.3.B69   1993   92-30727
635.9'09791'09154—dc20   CIP

British Library Cataloguing-in-Publication Data
A catalogue record for this book is available from the British Library.

Portions of this book have appeared in modified form in
Great Stream Review and *GreenPrints*.

2599

For my daughter, Heather Urry,

who wants a garden of her own someday,

and in memory of Mary Harder and Martha Bowers,

my gardening grandmothers

CONTENTS

PREFACE

My three-year-old garden is a small, suburban plot located squarely in the Sonoran Desert of southern Arizona. The location is crucial because, as every gardener knows, climate and soil determine what kinds of gardens we shall have— whether green lawns and flourishing rose beds or gravel paths and thrifty cacti. Location is crucial, too, in determining the garden's uninvited inhabitants: ruby-throated hummingbirds, raccoons, and silk moths in northeastern gardens, Anna's hummingbirds, horned lizards, and giant swallowtails in the Southwest. I myself started with nothing more than a few reliable vegetables and the easiest kinds of flowers, and ended up with green-tailed towhees, Leda's hairstreaks, Sonoran whiptails, and many more wild and half-wild creatures. It was not a garden so much as a menagerie, and if I tired of gardening, as I sometimes did, I knew that their welfare obliged me to continue.

From the beginning, I expected to watch biological principles at work in my garden, and indeed I did as mockingbirds battled above the trees, caterpillars transformed themselves into butterflies, and horned lizards snapped up ants. What

I didn't expect was that my garden would touch human knowledge at every possible point. History, philosophy, psychology, art, chemistry, anthropology, physics, horticulture, literature—volumes are there for the learning, and I'm frustrated at times by a mind too small to encompass it all.

This book reflects as much of my garden's diversity as possible. The first section, "The Garden and the Desert," illustrates the fruitful conjunction of biology and organic gardening. The second, "Ordinary Miracles," centers on garden wildlife, a variety of creatures whose common lives may provoke uncommon perceptions. "The Green Garden of the Heart," the third section, recognizes that if our gardens immeasurably complicate and enrich our lives, the reverse is also true. Any gardener has lived a lifetime in order to grow her garden.

In their entirety, these sixteen essays ask how we shall live, and recognize that before we can determine *how*, we need to find out *why*.

Thanks to all my gardening friends—Toni Yocum, Barbara Kingsolver, Jeanne Turner, Bob Webb, Tony Burgess, Nancy Ferguson, and Richard Felger—whose advice and knowledge became part of my garden. May their tomatoes set in March and their basil last until Christmas. Thanks too to Steve McLaughlin, Gary Nabhan, John Alcock, Barbara Kingsolver, Pamela Portwood, Kay Jimerson, Sandy Florence, Alison Moore, and Vera Norwood, whose encouragement and comments became part of this book.

The Garden and
the Desert

A GARDEN LIKE A LIFE

A garden, like a life, is composed of moments. I wish mine could always be as it is right now, this late afternoon at the end of March. Sunlight washes the upper branches of the mesquite tree. Orange cups of California poppy have closed for the day; white ones of evening primrose are about to open. Pink, white, lavender, purple, and cerise sweet peas quiver like butterflies tethered to a trellis. Wands of red-flowered penstemon bend under the probing of an Anna's hummingbird. Plump, black carpenter bees, shiny as patent leather shoes, steer toward the grapefruit tree, now a mass of stiff, white flowers. A breeze intermittently removes its fragrance, but between gusts the scent of my childhood drifts across the yard to me.

The first garden I remember, my paternal grandmother's, smelled like citrus blossoms, too. It seems that I can recall her garden in every detail until I try to grasp it. Then it fades into tantalizing shapes and colors and the hugeness of the spaces that a child sees. Mostly I remember row upon row of flowers, an immense expanse of blossoms it seemed then —dahlias, cosmos, roses, stocks, marigolds, marguerites, hollyhocks, phlox. I was afraid to walk among them because of the bees, and my heavy, slow-moving grandmother seemed a paragon of bravery as she stooped to pull weeds and cut deadheads. At the very back of the garden a row of sprawling blackberry vines exacted their tribute of blood in exchange for fruit. As I stood at the vines and looked back across the flowers and paths, the house seemed so far away I could conceivably get lost on the return trip.

Now I would love to be lost in such a garden. Mine is too small for that, though, so I lose myself in its moments instead. Seeing my garden as it is right now, I remember other moments at other times of year: the winter garden's tidy rows of broccoli, carrots, leeks, and beets; the summer garden's sprawling tomatoes and rambunctious melon vines. And I anticipate moments yet to come: when the first ripe tomato fills my mouth with the flavors of Italy and summertime, or when the mammoth sunflowers, now scrunched tightly like bunched paper bags, expand into upturned faces. Even though there's hardly a square centimeter of space left unplanted, I yearn to create as many moments as possible, to cram my garden to capacity or beyond, and I often stop by the nursery to thumb through the seed racks. Where in the world are you going to plant them? I ask myself every time my fingers close around a packet. Eventually, I escape with only one or two—golden zucchini for a fourth hill of squash, say, and purple beans for, well, someplace.

At the beginning, when my garden was new and thoughts of it agitated my days and dreams, I kept inviting friends to come and see my backyard paradise. They'd stroll the gravel paths, duly appreciative of the flowers and vegetables but never, it seemed to me, enthusiastic enough. Was this because my garden was actually rather dull? Or were they blind to its true beauty and real fascination? Finally, I realized that what makes my garden exciting is me. Living in it every day, participating minutely in each small event, I see with doubled and redoubled vision. Where friends notice a solitary hummingbird pricking the salvia flowers, I recall a season's worth of hummingbird battles. Where they see an ordinary mockingbird, I know a distinct individual whom I've studied as a forager, fighter, and performer. My friends, present in the garden only transiently, notice the surface prettiness, admire, and pass on to matters of more substance, while I see not merely the garden at this particular moment, but the garden as it has been at all other moments and as it will be in moments yet to come.

It astounds me still that I can succeed at gardening, as though the growing of food and flowers should be so arcane that only an alchemist could carry it off. "Of course, I won't be very good at gardening. My garden won't look nice. It won't produce well." Those ideas were firmly in place at the beginning, and it's startling to find they're not true.

Even though I've been a professional botanist for more than a decade, I never intended to have a garden. For years, in fact, I was content with my quixotic image as a botanist who couldn't grow plants, and when friends, hoping for a diagnosis, described their yellowing philodendrons or spotted ficus benjamimas, I would shrug apologetically and say, "I'm not that kind of botanist." Wild plants were my passion, and I took more interest in the weeds at the curb than in the bed of chrysanthemums three feet away. But wherever passion exists, the energy for transformation exists, too, and it was almost inevitable that I'd eventually become a gardener.

Or perhaps my garden represents less the imperatives of fate than the workings of mere chronology, which, like biology, can sometimes be destiny. As a friend of a friend ambiguously replied when asked if she gardened, "If you can call it that. Forty is about the age for that sort of thing, isn't it?" She was right. Forty is about the age for unexpected developments: extroverts turn introspective, introverts become sociable, and everyone, without regard to type, acquires gray hairs and philosophies of life. Many also acquire gardens.

If I close my eyes, I can remember what this space looked like before: a stubble of dead bermuda grass on parched earth, patches of weeds according to season, a sunburned hedge on one side of the yard, stumps of dead grapevine on the other. All it needed to complete the picture was a broken-down car on blocks. I was not unwilling for this state of affairs to continue indefinitely, and, one day, when without a word of preamble or explanation, my husband outlined a flower bed on the stubbled dirt, the main question in my mind was, "How in the world are we going to fill that enormous space?" A garden seemed as unlikely as a Tasmanian devil, and all my husband's grubbing out of moribund shrubbery and laying of drip-irrigation lines represented nothing more than the great masculine tradition of yard work. Certainly it held no potential interest for me. After all, I wasn't that kind of botanist.

But I couldn't very well sit indoors reading a book while he labored alone with shovel, wheelbarrow, hoe, and rake. Human courtesy (not to mention matrimonial harmony) demanded that I assist. Just as the throwing of a stick triggers a retriever's fetching instinct, so the sinking of a spade into dirt released some native instinct in me. By the time the bed was dug, the drip lines laid, the paths graveled, I had graduated from assistant to partner. My husband, who knows a chronological imperative when he sees one, stepped aside at that point, and by the time the earth was fertilized and the first rows planted, I had become both head gardener and chief assistant, too. And I stuck with it. That still amazes me. I stayed with my garden.

By all previous indications, I should have been a temporary gardener, one of those for whom gardening is nothing more than another way of filling time, like painting ceramic figurines or arranging artificial flowers. But we don't give up on the things we are meant to do, which is another way of saying that the passion we bring to our activities won't allow us to quit them. What made me stick with my garden was not so much the digging (although I loved the crumble of clods between my fingers) or the produce (although I valued every single tomato, pea, green bean, and cantaloupe) or even the multiplicity of living creatures drawn by the miniature world I'd half created, half evoked. The reason I stayed in gardening was all of these combined, especially their unfolding as unexpectedly as the twists and turns of a life.

When I was a child, I would lie in bed at night and imagine all the rooms of the house in place around me: the living room just behind my head, the coat closet behind my bookshelf, the hallway to my right, my sister's room beyond my toes: every space in its exact and somewhat mysterious relation to every other space, the walls opaque to the eye but penetrable by the imagination, the whole forming a three-dimensional blueprint that represented the known and the unknown, the security of home and the possibility of explorations beyond its familiar perimeter.

In much the same way I now like to imagine my garden in its place in the neighborhood, the city, the surrounding desert. The centermost of these concentric rings is my back-yard, a rectangle some eighty feet long and half as wide, bounded on one side by an unkempt pyracantha hedge and a tall board fence, on the other by a chain-link fence loosely embroidered with vines. The far end terminates at a spreading mesquite tree that volunteered long ago in the weedy alley, and the near end stops at my back door. Beyond these bound-aries lie other yards, unknown except for brief glimpses from the roof or through fences, yards where swimming pools or patrolling dogs take the place of gardens, where blue morning glories riot over sunflowers and bermuda grass clutches straggling tomato plants, where potted cacti fatten on a diet of occasional water and constant sun. One after another, separated by tall hedges or block walls or wooden fences, these yards and gardens proliferate across the valley floor, each set into the grid of city streets and drainage channels, each occupying its own inviolate space yet joined by an underground network of pipes and an overhead web of wires, spilling at last onto the ragged margins of the desert. Here, where even bermuda grass hesitates and none of the cacti are in pots, we realize the utter artificiality of all that lies inside.

You'd think we could be satisfied with the desert's own peculiar beauty and abundance, especially in the rare springs when winter rains start early and countless wildflowers soften the angular slopes. Then the desert is a garden in itself. Even in the hottest, driest months, when wildflowers are a memory or a wish and an outdoor stroll is more penance than pleasure, the desert still looks something like a garden. On plains, the sparsely leaved creosote bushes space themselves as precisely as topiary in the great gardens at Versailles, and on foothills, the twiggy canopies of paloverde trees provide massed greenery in the distance. Cacti, placed just so about the landscape, could be garden statuary, especially the magnificent saguaros that poke well above the trees. A variety of indistinguishable gray shrubs would be suitable, if properly trimmed, to edge sidewalks and flower beds.

But evidently the desert itself is not garden enough. Bred to artificial climates and artificial landscapes, we want clearer distinctions and firmer boundaries for our lives.

The native vegetation here survives on ten or eleven inches of rainfall a year, part in winter, the rest in summer. Some years it makes do with much less. Then, even the saguaros, which normally contain up to a ton of water, suffer visibly as their skin shrivels between the vertical ribs until they look like half-starved dogs. We city gardeners take whatever water nature provides and add to it some thirty inches more, water withdrawn from ancient aquifers formed during wetter times. At two cents a cubic foot, water is generally the most expensive component of our gardens, and we use it as wisely as possible, even while admitting that the wisest choice would be not to use it all.

We compromise by disassembling the conventional garden into its components, tucking the parts wherever they fit: a narrow bed along the fence might hold three melon vines, a planter under the bedroom window could be an asparagus bed, the unused strip beside the house should be fine for tomatoes, and almost any place will do for the two or three eggplant bushes that more than satisfy the needs of most households. Even the lushest desert gardens show some space of bare ground since a continuous cover of green is morally indefensible as well as economically impractical.

In this way, the desert defines, determines, and delimits. The gardens that bloom so beautifully in our minds, the ones where zinnias never die of wilt and summer days are never so hot that delicate leaves turn crisp and brown, these gardens are the Platonic ideal. The gardens we're actually stuck with, the ones where green beans drop before they're the size of matchsticks, corn plants topple in thunderstorms and summer balsam germinates but never blooms, these gardens correspond to real life. This is the garden I have made, the garden where I must live. Its virtues are my own; its faults and limitations are mine, too. It exists at my forbearance, and without my constant attention, it will die—perish all the quicker because I garden in the desert, and if a garden is an expression of personality, it is just as much an expression of place.

STOLEN WATER

"Water being available, a garden is inevitable," says Donald N. Wilbur. Desert gardeners realize the truth of this most strongly in April and May. That's when, as if by some cosmic law of compensation, city gardens flourish while the desert garden languishes. Out there, pads of prickly pear shrivel from heat and drought. Joints of staghorn cholla turn maroon, a response to stress. Brittlebush, a hemisphere of blue-green leaves after winter rains, is reduced to its essence, a few white stems and withered leaves too tired to fall off. Wolfberry becomes a collection of dead-looking twigs and thorns. Birds and animals participate in the overall retreat, restricting their activities to the coolness of early morning or evening. Only insects seem immune to midday temperatures: wasps cruise slowly and silently over leafless branches, and cicadas whine like steel guitars.

Meanwhile, a few miles away in the well-watered paradise of the city garden, sweet peas and Iceland poppies have already succumbed to the rising curve of summer, but petunias straggle on despite the heat, and cosmos, zinnia, verbena, coreopsis, salvia, and sunflower flourish, a gaudy spatter painting in reds, yellows, magentas, and pinks. Oleanders, even neglected ones, flower with abandon—billows of white, pink, magenta, and maroon on every street and in every park. Tomatoes flush orange, then vermilion, then red, that sexy, tempting crimson that indicates perfect ripeness, surely the exact color that caused so much trouble in the Garden of Eden. Melon vines gallop across paths and passageways, so exuberant you can almost hear them shout. Their tiny green ovaries, swathed in silver fur, promise sweetness later on.

By June it's so hot that tomato vines won't set fruit. Vegetables and flowers become painfully thirsty in the desiccating heat and require irrigation every other day. My cat spends the daylight hours flopped on a shady patch of damp earth. This seems a sensible solution to me, and I often wish that I could reverse day and night for the duration of the summer. These are the days when I garden early in the morning before the day turns into a dazzle of heat and glare. At this predawn hour, the sky is always spongy and gray, as though congested with clouds, and I pretend to wonder what kind of day it will be, as if it or I had a choice. Of course, the arrival of the sun brings a milky blue sky without a cloud in it; the day will be faultlessly sunny like the day before and the day to come. Every day in this season is much like its companions, and time seems suspended in heat.

What we are waiting for is clouds. Borne on a tongue of moist air that slips northward from the Gulf of Mexico, they come about the middle of June. There's no rain in them at first, but at least they bring a promise of change. We keep a hopeful eye on the dewpoint, the temperature at which the air is saturated with moisture. Slowly it rises, from forty degrees at the end of May to fifty degrees by the end of June.

The magic number is sixty: at sixty degrees, the saturated atmosphere will spill its contents to the earth, announcing the arrival of the summer rainy season.

If I'm indoors, the first rain always surprises me: only when I peek outside do I connect the peculiar rustling in the palm fronds with big drops of rain plopping down at widely spaced intervals. All through July and August distant storms color the sky like a bruise, a wonderful, frightening, brooding color. I watch their approach with joy and foreboding. Silver threads of lightning flicker from clouds to ground, and thunder booms like distant drums. Drawing closer, it bangs like an entire load of lumber being dumped on the ground all at once. Wind whips the treetops and hurls newspapers and plastic bags high into the sky. Then rain descends, thick as nails poured from a hopper.

The desert responds immediately: within forty-eight hours of the first heavy storm, leaf buds sprout on thorny bare stems of ocotillo; within a week, fat flower buds erupt from creosote-bush twigs; within a month, rocky slopes are vivid with morning glories, summer poppies, devil's claw, portulaca, and half a dozen kinds of annual grasses. Desert tortoises amble out of hibernation in search of soft, green things to eat. Millipedes waver across the soil, green fig beetles saw through the air, dragonflies perform loop-the-loops above the paloverdes, now flush with tiny leaflets.

By watering city gardens continually, we maintain them in a state of artificial summer from May to October, so the arrival of the rains has no such marked, startling effect. Garden plants love the humidity, though; it offers them momentary surcease from the summer-long struggle to preserve their tissues in a turgid state. Otherwise, the garden is much as it was before the rains started except that I become more keenly aware of time's passing. Already, in the midst of bounteous tomatoes, I think sadly of the days ahead when they'll be gone. It's the summer garden that brings out this feeling most strongly—the sweet pungency of basil, the mellow succulence of melon, none of these can be kept past their time. Summer gardening is a lesson in letting go.

In September, we let go of the summer rains as the moist air retreats southward, abandoning us to a second season of hot and cloudless days, an arid aftersummer that passes for autumn only because it precedes the winter. Now, while the days are still uncomfortably warm, we must prepare our winter gardens, a salient peculiarity of the desert gardener's life. While gardeners elsewhere ease into a well-deserved rest, we shovel bags of manure over bare ground, dig it in, water it well, and plant it with the usual mixture of anxiety and hope. Seeds germinate quickly in the warm soil, and in sixty days or so we will be picking our first snow peas and chard.

Winter rains, if we're lucky enough to get any, start in November and continue sporadically into March. These gentle, soaking rains are the dregs of widespread storms blown in from the Pacific Ocean. Frost is a regular occurrence, and during cold snaps, the tenderest gardens lie half-hidden under tarpaulins and bedsheets. Those daring gardeners who set out tomato plants in late February must be ready to shelter them under bags and boxes until the middle of March or even later. Many desert plants—cacti, acacias and certain others with tropical affinities—don't respond to winter rain at all since their roots won't take up water from cold soil, but garden crops like broccoli, lettuce, peas, carrots, beets, chard and spinach flourish under this regime of chilly nights and mild days.

During the winter, my garden seems a fairy-tale place, one under an enchantment of silence. Other than the cat and a few resident birds, there's little animal life. No butterflies, few bees, some pillbugs and earwigs in the compost pile, too many aphids. The spell is broken in late January by lengthening days. Cats court, birds sing, poppy buds nod on thick stalks. In the middle of February, the first carpenter bees and butterflies arrive, and within a few weeks, insect populations boom.

During March, desert and city gardens become synchronized at last. In the desert, California poppies burn orange on rocky slopes. Yellow and lavender mats of bladderpod and filaree spread across barren ground. Blue lupines flow along road shoulders and trickle down the embankments. In town, the provident gardeners, the ones who spent the best days of autumn on their knees in the garden, now glory in borders of pansy, stock, delphinium, poppy, snapdragon, ranunculus, and anemone. The rest of us scramble to the nursery for quick-growing transplants. There's hardly a yard so mean that it doesn't have potted petunias spilling onto the front porch or a row of pansies along the sidewalk. Suddenly everybody feels like gardening, and the nurseries swarm with customers. Already we have forgotten how painfully thirsty the garden becomes in summer.

March makes it easy to ignore the desert around us; May won't let us forget. The desert reminds us that spring, a beginning almost everywhere else, is an end here. The rare and glorious displays of spring wildflowers will die as the soil dries out. The shrubs and trees will drop their leaves and leaflets. Spring leads to nothing but its own demise as every living plant and animal retreats against the heat and drought of early summer. Except in town, of course, where gardeners rich in borrowed water can circumscribe new boundaries for their lives.

And so it's May, and even though the sun has not yet risen, the coming heat of the day is apparent in the heaviness of the air. The eastern horizon is pale, as if white-hot. Stepping outdoors, I see that other gardeners are out and about, too.

The white-haired woman who lives across the street bends down slowly to place a whirly-bird sprinkler in the geometric center of her lawn. Down the block, a wiry old man in suspenders and an undershirt sprinkles a peach tree from a hose. The water arches into the air and falls as separate droplets, each as precious as oil, you might think, or even saffron. Yet, at this season, nearly two months since our last rain, the water we receive from spigots and hoses via pumps and pipes is not quite that precious. It costs one-fifth of a cent per gallon, which equals one-fortieth of a cent per pound. Saffron, when I can locate any, is $355 per ounce.

The old man with the peach tree lives behind one of two city wells in our neighborhood. The well itself—city well number four—is a hidden shaft several hundred feet deep; what I see above ground is a huge, cylindrical tank buttressed by pipes. For a while I fondly believed that this particular well supplied the water that came out of my tap. On behalf of my tomatoes and watermelons, I'd give it a little salute whenever I passed. It's a good thing, I used to tell myself, to know where your water comes from when you live in the desert.

One day, however, I had occasion to call the city water department, and I learned that I was completely wrong. "It doesn't work that way," said the engineer who took my call. "All the wells in your area pump water into collector lines and reservoirs. Individual households draw from this pooled water. During shortages, some of the water you use could be coming from as far away as Avra Valley."

Oh.

Now, every time I walk by city well number four, from which my household water explicitly does *not* come, I think about the village wells I saw in West Africa. These are wells you can actually see, deep shafts surrounded by cement collars. When you peer inside at noon, gleams of light dance across the blackness far below. Several times a day the village women, swathed in brilliantly colored cotton prints, gather at the well, where they drink friendship as well as water. They lower wooden buckets into the shaft, then, muscles straining, haul them back up again. The well is an umbilical cord that connects them directly and intimately to their life-support system.

The ancient Persians, who lived on arid and treeless plateaus, knew where their water came from, too. At the base of a snow-capped mountain, they would sink a shaft to the water table, then construct a tunnel, called a *qanat*, between the shaft and their village. Some qanats were miles long. Near the outskirts of the village, the qanat surfaced as a network of open canals feeding fields, orchards, mill wheels, and, inevitably, gardens. Every garden had its pool, always constructed on the slightest of slopes so that the water would brim and overflow into narrow channels that irrigated flower beds and shady walks. Gardeners sometimes floated petals on the pools to make elaborate designs like oriental carpets. At night, they might set candles adrift on tiny rafts. No wonder their word for garden also meant paradise.

The Tohono O'odham, immemorial inhabitants of the Arizona desert, lacked the means to construct qanats. They had no access to deep underground water until 1912, when Anglos introduced drilling rigs and wells. Before then the O'odham had no more water than a coyote or a cactus. Living in a land of unreliable water holes and ephemeral streams, they knew perfectly well where their water came from: "By the sandy water I breathe in the odor of the sea," they chanted, "from there clouds come and rain falls over the world." They saw it for themselves on their annual salt treks to the Gulf of California. There it was—tomorrow's weather—welling up from the ocean, manufactured over that restless sheet of water and dispatched toward land.

Sometimes when I sprinkle my garden, I remember that the water coming out of the hose probably fell as raindrops ten thousand years ago. Back then, conifer woodlands grew where cactus thrives now and annual rainfall was twice or even three times as great as today, great enough, anyway, that permanent streams flowed where we have only sandy washes now. This land was then an active participant in the hydrological cycle. Rivers like the Salt and the Gila flowed all the way to the Colorado River, which in turn debouched into the Gulf of California, which in turn boiled up clouds that delivered rain far into the interior, enough rain to saturate the aquifers—porous beds of sandstone, silt and conglomerate—that underlie the city where I live.

If this ancient water source were visible as mineralized fossils on the land surface, we would probably declare it a national park, set it aside for veneration and admiration. Instead we draw upon it as casually as we draw upon the atmosphere for the oxygen we breathe: 150 gallons per person per day on the average. We choose to forget these facts: that we live in a desert, that a good year brings only twelve inches of rain, that generous amounts of water percolate into the aquifer only in years of above-average rainfall, that there are many more bad years than good.

Most of the recharge to the Tucson basin comes from streamflow: after storms, the washes run for an hour or two, then dry up. Some of this water evaporates, some runs out of the basin, some is used by plants and some—82,000 acre-feet a year—percolates into the water table. Until the 1950s, our withdrawals from the aquifer approximately equalled the recharge from natural rainfall. Now our three hundred city wells withdraw 300,000 acre-feet a year, nearly four times as much as nature recharges. We know where our water comes from, all right, but evidently we don't care.

When you've hauled up a thirty-pound bucket from a fifty-foot-deep shaft or walked sixteen miles every day to the nearest source of water or constructed a five-mile-long qanat one shovelful of dirt at a time, you do care. There's no question then of where your water comes from, every drop of it, or of exactly what its value is. This is the stuff of poetry made visible. Try as I might, I can see precious little poetry connected with city well number four, which is all machinery and electricity and pressurization. Whatever poetry exists is hidden far beneath my feet, way down where the groundwater silently flows in secret channels.

When I started gardening, I thought of water in purely economic terms. Our water may be cheaper than saffron, but it's still costly enough that we have water thieves—folks who divert household water so it won't flow through their meters. (One man actually filled an entire swimming pool with stolen water.) My first water bill was higher than I expected—twice as much as usual—but not high enough to make me cover my garden with plastic and pea gravel, a common solution to high water bills here. My friend Margaret, who finally gave up her desert garden, tells me that once you figure out the cost of water, fertilizers, and sprays, the price per vegetable is surprisingly high. Only if your garden is extremely productive can you beat supermarket prices, she insists. Moreover, she points out, productivity in desert gardens drops precipitously in July and August, when the water demands of garden plants are at their highest; yet, to benefit from renewed productivity in the fall, you must continue to water as if your vegetables were producing at their peak.

Anxious to discover whether she was right or wrong, I calculated my costs for the first summer of gardening and discovered that I made a slight profit on tomatoes and melons. As if that mattered. As if the fact that homegrown watermelons are cheaper than store-bought has anything to do with whether or not a desert garden can be justified. When it comes right down to it, the question of whether or not to have a garden in a land of little water is not an economic but a moral one. Where water is precious, every frivolous use is thievery.

Old photographs show that early settlers here—the Spaniards and Mexicans—set their houses amid creosote bush and cactus. They lived in a desert and didn't try to hide that fact from themselves. It wasn't until later that homesick Anglos, trying to recreate New England in the middle of the desert, planted lawns and shade trees with little thought of when the water might run out. Their attitude still dominates local landscaping. My friend Carl, head groundskeeper at a posh resort on the edge of town, applied for work at a larger, even posher resort. He showed his prospective employer some cactus plantings he had designed. The plantings were attractive, diverse, and, of course, water-sparing.

"Oh, no," he was told, "that will never do. We don't like the desert look."

I do. But I like having a garden, too. If I grow thirsty plants like zucchini and watermelon, am I living as if water mattered? I offer trade-offs to salve my conscience. What if I take a shower every other day instead of daily? What if I wash my car only once a month—or never? Shouldn't it be permissible to grow vegetables if I don't have a lawn? If I build up the soil with compost, it will retain more water, and I'll need to irrigate less often. At least I dig my garden by hand; I'm not pouring irreplaceable fossil fuels into a gasoline-powered rototiller. Oh, I turn cartwheels in my efforts to rationalize this desert garden.

I am not accustomed to denying myself. Ours is a society of abundance. We have no "painful moon," which, for the Tohono O'odham, was the month of May, a lean time when the food produced by winter rains had been consumed and the summer downpours were still a month or more away.

The plenitude of goods in our stores never varies, and our landfills bulge with articles that, in a less profligate society, would be recycled until every molecule had been abraded away. We have so much we can waste three-fourths of it and never notice.

The Tohono O'odham lived in a society of abundance, too, but not in the same sense that we do. "Having little," as Charles Bowden noted, "they shared all." A deer hunter returning to his village with a buck did not regard it as his deer alone. His hunting skills belonged to everyone, and everyone benefited by trading beans or corn for venison. Sharing with one another, they evened out the wild lottery of nature, which could be bountiful one season, miserly the next. Even in the rainy seasons, they used water and other resources respectfully. In their particular society of abundance, waste was unthinkable.

Thoughts of water and abundance go hand in hand when you live in a desert. I think them often in the garden, especially when I discover cucumbers grown too large to be eaten or tomatoes too decayed to turn into sauce. If I toss these far-gone vegetables into the compost bin, I feel that I'm not wasting them as baldly as if I threw them into the garbage can to be hauled to the landfill. But it would have been better still had I harvested them at the point of perfection and turned them into a salad or some other delicious dish. By growing more vegetables than I can eat, I create waste and steal water.

I haven't given up my garden yet. For now, I am more careful than I once was to grow just enough, no more. If twenty-seven bush bean plants suffice, that's how many seeds I sow. If six tomato vines are enough, why plant eight? Ours might not always be a society of abundance. The day might come when we cannot afford to let each person drive her own car to the office or heat her house to an even seventy-five degrees all winter long. Desert dwellers might not always be able to have gardens. When that day comes—if it does—I hope I can bow gracefully to necessity. Until then, I watch the sky for rain and the sandy washes for recharge. I know where my water comes from.

THE GARDENER'S SHADOW

The best fertilizer is the gardener's own shadow.

OLD CHINESE PROVERB

"Start with anything, end up with bermuda." That's what horticulture professors say about lawns in desert towns. Dichondra, winter rye, St. Augustine, even plain old pea gravel—all are eventually crowded out and supplanted by bermuda grass, which assaults from below with creeping rhizomes and from above with wind-borne seed and leaping stems. My father used to call it devil grass, the perfect name for it.

Having constructed my garden on the ragged remnants of a bermuda grass lawn, I discovered for myself what a hardy enemy it could be. Although most of its rhizomes lay within six inches of the surface, some penetrated to eighteen inches, nearly beyond the reach of my shovel. Eradicating my lawn one clump at a time was slow work. As I dug, I shook each clump free of dirt, then dropped it into a box or bucket. I often stopped to comb the loose dirt with my fingers to make certain I had not overlooked even the tiniest rhizome. If by some chance I did, I would know about it in a week or two when new leaves poked above the ground. It always amazed me that, without benefit of photosynthetic tissue, these bits of stem had the power to grow and differentiate even when buried under a foot of dirt and darkness. They must be starchy, like tubers and bulbs, which also put forth rootlets and pale, blind shoots that unerringly seek the light.

Local experts prescribe an easy if expensive solution to bermuda grass: Doomsday, an herbicide containing glyphosate as its active ingredient. A single application of Doomsday sprayed on actively growing grass will rid your garden of bermuda forever, they promise. Except that it doesn't. Over my protests, my husband faithfully poisoned the bermuda grass in our alley according to prescription. Its leaves turned brown and died, and that, we thought, was the end of it. When the summer rains started, though, it was not doomsday but resurrection day as some of the clumps turned green and overran the alley with tentacles a yard long.

Secretly pleased that the chemists, professors, and husbands had failed, I was back at my old task of prying out bermuda grass with a shovel, whereupon I made the startling discovery that even the ostensibly dead clumps were only playing possum. Underground their rhizomes thrived, some so thick and succulent and pale that they reminded me of French asparagus carefully blanched in mounded dirt. Soon they, too, would be feeling their way toward the rich soil and abundant moisture of my garden.

Start with anything, sooner or later you'll end up with bermuda grass. If the nearest source is your next-door neighbor's lawn, you'll get it sooner. One summer, as I dug bermuda in the narrow alley that separates our two yards, my neighbor peered over his fence long enough to say, "I tried that earlier this summer. It just comes back."

Well, I'd seen him at work, and I knew for a fact that he merely pulled the tops off at ground level. "You have to dig up the roots," I said, "or it *will* come back." I didn't add, as I might have, that I had successfully eliminated bermuda grass from the alley the previous summer, nor did I point out that the present crop had reinvaded from his yard, nor did I imply that my present labor was a direct consequence of his shiftlessness.

We don't see eye to eye on much, my neighbor and I, especially when it comes to gardens. I'm reluctant to call *his* a garden at all, that patch of brown dirt in one corner of his yard. A shabby wood fence marks the north side, and a wobbly length of chicken wire bounds the remainder of the plot. A half-dead mulberry tree serves mainly as a backstop for the heap of rubbish that serves, I would guess, as a compost pile, although how he expects it to rot in this hot, dry climate if he neither waters nor turns it is beyond me. His severely utilitarian plot contains tomatoes, zucchini, pumpkin, and bermuda grass, nothing else. No flowers, no ornamentals of any sort. Its sole function is to provide vegetables, not pleasure, and when in the evenings, hands on hips, he surveys his plantings, he looks more like Napoleon passing his troops in review than a mother watching her baby as it sleeps.

It's not just the compost pile he mismanages. He works the soil when it's wet, then lets the clods dry rock hard. Instead of digging out the invading bermuda grass, he yanks out handfuls of leaf and stem as though that solved the problem. He turns up his nose at manure, preferring the odorless, gunmetal gray pellets of ammonium phosphate that do nothing to lighten our heavy clay soils. Since he grows no flowers, his garden attracts few of the beneficial insects—bees, wasps, ladybugs, and lacewings—that love flowery places and do half a gardener's work for her. By default, he must resort to pesticides, and this I cannot forgive. As I said, we don't agree on much.

I knew from the start that mine would be an organic garden even though the usual rationalizations for organic gardening left me unconvinced. I could see no particular reason to favor organic fertilizers over chemical ones since, as far as plants are concerned, nitrate molecules synthesized by Dow Chemical Company are identical to the natural ones present in steer manure. I doubted that, as organic gardeners claimed, chemical fertilizers kill beneficial soil organisms, thereby making plants susceptible to disease and requiring use of pesticides and more chemical fertilizers. Data, I said, let's see some data. I distrusted, too, what struck me as the lunatic fringe of organic gardening, the New Age types who plant according to phases of the moon and insist that carrots love tomatoes. Despite these misgivings, the underlying principle of organic gardening—to create a functioning, self-regulating ecosystem in your own backyard—appealed strongly to the biologist in me. I understood that home gardens belong to a larger network of farms, green belts, and open country, a natural environment that supports life by producing food, recycling water, assimilating wastes, and purifying air. Cities and towns, with their grids of asphalt, concrete, glass, and steel, make no food, purify no air, clean little water. They are parasites. Without the healing and beneficial effects of the natural environment, cities would quickly perish in their own excreta.

As a biologist—and presumably a lover of life in all its forms—I also liked the idea of living in peace with my garden. Moreover, as a consumer of far too many pesticide-laden vegetables and fruits from the grocery store, I could see no reason to increase the load.

All this was clear from the beginning, as I said. What wasn't clear was how to go about it. My initial harvest—six pitiful, gnarly carrots and a handful of tasteless green beans—proved that simply poking seeds into the ground wasn't enough.

A librarian's daughter, I turned, as usual, to books, where I discovered that my first guesses were right in some respects, wrong in others. Nitrogen is indeed nitrogen no matter what its source, but it is also true that, as organic gardeners claim, a diet of chemical nitrogen does not promote healthy, vital soil. As one agronomist puts it, soil is not just another instrument of production, like pesticides, fertilizers, or tractors. It is, rather, a complex, fragile medium for life. A tablespoon of soil contains millions of grains of sand, silt, and clay. Each grain presents multiple surfaces to which plant nutrients can adhere. Individual grains are tiny, but taken together, their surface area—and potential for supplying nutrients—is huge.

Billions of bacteria, fungi, and algae live in that same tablespoon of soil. They invisibly turn organic matter into humus, one of the most useful substances on the face of the earth. That's why biointensive gardeners like John Jeavons emphasize that soil can die if mistreated. "Be sure to realize that you are watering *the soil*, not the plant," he urges. "Keeping the soil *alive* will retain water best and minimize the water consumed." As organic gardeners have long known, soils rich in humus are also rich in plant nutrients. Humus-laden soils resist erosion better, too, because the microorganisms manufacture polysaccharides, which glue the soil particles together.

Bit by bit, I pieced together a system that worked for me. Beds level with the ground surface and irrigated with soaker hoses. Abundant applications of steer manure at the start of the growing season with occasional side dressings of compost and fish emulsion thereafter. Compost in a bin cobbled together with chicken wire, boards, and a staple gun. *Bacillus thuringiensis*, a bacterial disease in a bottle, for caterpillars; a hot sauce made from water, soap, and red chiles for aphids; and handpicking (or handwringing) for almost everything else.

Often I discovered that problems weren't really problems. If flea beetles perforated my turnip leaves until they looked like they had been peppered with buckshot, what did it matter? I didn't plan to eat the leaves, so the insects did me no real harm. If small green grasshoppers gnawed holes in my tomatoes, at least they never ate the entire fruit, which was admittedly unsightly but no less flavorful for that. If paper wasps stole nectar from the hummingbird feeder, wasn't this a small price to pay in return for all the caterpillars they harvested? If curve-billed thrashers yanked seedlings out of the ground, they also ate the soil-dwelling grubs that chew on roots. Even my old enemy bermuda grass did some good: its extensive system of roots and rhizomes added organic matter to the soil and provided food for earthworms.

This attitude—that everything that seems like a problem isn't necessarily one—is really the essence of organic gardening. Organic gardeners are, by and large, large-hearted people. They are able to accept an imperfect world, or, better yet, they are willing to entertain the idea that a perfect world includes tomato hornworms as well as tomatoes and cucumber beetles as well as cucumbers. Because of this, most organic gardeners distrust the good bug–bad bug dichotomy. The inorganic gardener who reaches for the Malathion inarguably succeeds in killing the "bad" bugs: the cucumber beetles that carry bacterial wilt, the leafhopper bugs that carry tomato viruses, the entire panoply of gnawing, sucking, chewing insects that thrive in the artificial Eden of the desert garden. But for every cucumber beetle he slays, he inadvertently kills a dozen honeybees, and who will pollinate his cucumbers then?

The home gardener with his aerosol guns of toxic sprays mimics the large-scale farmer who hires crop dusters to spray the same chemicals over a much larger area. It's a painful irony that in doing so, farmers actually multiply their problems. Applying insecticides over large areas produces insects that are highly resistant to poisons. It works this way. Most of the sprayed insects die, but a few survive, mate with one another, and pass along their pesticide-resistant genes to their offspring. The heavier the rate of pesticide application, the more rapidly resistant strains evolve. Since pesticides kill natural predators, too, the now-resistant pest population booms. Not only are there as many pests as before, they no longer respond to the same chemical formula. The inorganic farmer is his own worst enemy.

Thanks to organic gardeners (and anyone who eschews chemical controls), this is unlikely to happen on a neighborhood scale. Even in a neighborhood where most gardeners control insect pests with toxic sprays, a few organic gardeners will have a positive impact all out of proportion to their numbers and the size of their gardens. The pesticide-free zones become refuges for susceptible pests—the lucky ones who should have been killed but managed to escape somehow. Mating with one another and with resistant pests, they contribute their susceptible genes to the population, thus retarding the evolution of pesticide-resistant strains.

Gardening is applied biology, as my friend Tony is fond of saying. To be an organic gardener is simply to be a good biologist. Everyone knows about ladybugs (or, more properly, lady beetles), that the larvae eat twenty to fifty aphids a day, that the adults consume twice that and eat as many as one hundred aphid eggs daily, too. The good biologist also knows about lacewings, delicate green-winged insects whose larvae look like miniature crocodiles and have appetites to match. A single lacewing larva eats some two hundred aphids between the time it hatches and the time it pupates. Since the female lays more than six hundred eggs in her brief lifetime, simple mathematics suggest that the smart gardener should cosset lacewings, not poison them with insecticides or electrocute them in light traps. Even professional agronomists and entomologists, often little more than shills for the pesticide industry that funds their research, recognize that natural predators, like paper wasps, can be an effective substitute for chemical poisons.

As an applied biologist, the organic gardener knows that lacewings, ladybugs, paper wasps, honeybees, earthworms, and other beneficial animals don't exist in a vacuum. Like every living creature they have needs, and the smart gardener supplies as many of them as possible. Soil that is rich in organic matter is a paradise for earthworms, who do yeoman's work in turning and aerating the soil. The best thing a gardener can do is give them plenty of food—rotted manure, compost, even fresh kitchen wastes. A small fish pond, a delightful thing in itself, furnishes water for paper wasps and honeybees. Among the most voracious harvesters of insect pests are birds with nestlings—a pair of mockingbirds might feed their young more than three thousand insects over a twelve-day period—and the intelligent gardener entices nesting birds by providing trees, shrubs, and a thriving insect population. Undoubtedly, the smartest thing a gardener can do is foster as much diversity as possible. A diverse fauna ensures a rich array of natural predators—paper and ichneumon wasps for caterpillars, ammophila wasps for crickets and grasshoppers, ladybugs and lacewings for aphids, mockingbirds and cactus wrens for everything else. When many insects share the garden, no single kind (except, perhaps, for aphids) can predominate: there simply isn't enough physical space.

The best way to ensure a diverse fauna is to cultivate a diverse flora. Monocultures—unending fields of wheat or corn or sorghum—are a recent idea, one geared to the economics of the marketplace, which encourages efficiency in planting, fertilizing, and harvesting. In parts of the world where mechanization has yet to arrive, farm fields look more like home gardens—polycultures that, like Virginia Woolf's diary, are elastic enough to hold a number of things without strain. The O'odham peoples of central and southern Arizona, for instance, lavishly edged their hand-dug irrigation canals with native trees and shrubs. Thickets of vegetation surrounded the fields, too, and big shade trees like mesquites were left standing. Crops like corn and beans were intermingled, often in the company of weeds like amaranth and purslane.

These Native Americans farmed according to the economy of nature, not the economy of the marketplace. Living without the dubious benefits of chemical fertilizers and pesticides, they relied on organic techniques. Diverting humus-laden floodwaters boosted the fertility of their fields, as did animal manure and the nitrogen-rich litter from mesquite trees. Thickets of mesquite, graythorn, wolfberry, and salt-bush along the canals and fields, by attracting a variety of birds and insects, ensured a wide array of natural predators for crop pests. These hedgerows also yielded edible fruits in season. Many so-called weeds were eaten as greens. Others provided shade for crops and soil. Interplanting made efficient use of space: sturdy corn stalks gave support to climbing bean plants, and the beans supplied nitrogen to the corn.

Organic gardeners have been pointing all this out for years with little result. Professional agronomists ridiculed the idea of companion planting and ignored the existence of natural predators. Home gardeners, turning to their local agricultural extension service for guidance, learned about chemical controls like Malathion and Sevin rather than biological ones like *Bacillus thuringiensis*. Recently, however, a new generation of agronomists and ecologists, many of them young iconoclasts raised on the environmental renaissance of the sixties and seventies, has brought scientific rigor to the organic gardening movement. Growing broccoli or cucumbers in mono-culture and in mixed cultures, they have discovered what organic gardeners knew all along: the number of pests is any-where from ten to thirty times as great in the monoculture. (Good, solid data at last.) Specialist insects readily exploit the simple system of a monoculture but are baffled when it comes to the complexities of the polyculture. The clash of odors in a patch where tomato, collards, and tarragon are grown side by side makes it harder for flea beetles to track the perfume that they prefer.

Of course, an organic garden is more work than an in-organic one—more work to plant, more work to maintain, more work to harvest. The small, green caterpillars that feed on my snow peas do so not out in the open, where they'd be vulnerable to predators (including me), but stitched in-side the topmost pair of bracts. To control them with *Bacillus thuringiensis*, I must pry apart and spray each pair of bracts individually. To keep my corn plants from toppling in high winds, I must shovel loose dirt around the base of each one. This encourages the growth of adventitious roots that but-tress the stalks. To keep aphid populations under control, I must spray them with hot sauce, not just once but several times, and in between sprayings I must keep checking the plants for reinfestations. All this takes time and effort and the attitude that the best fertilizer is the gardener's own shadow.

In a way, this attitude is both a means and an end. It be-comes its own reward, as close as most of us will ever get to the reverence that Native Americans feel toward their crops and fields. The Hopi Indians, inhabitants of a land where rainfall is scanty and irregular and the growing season short, treat corn with as much delicacy and respect as a Catholic does the Eucharist. The ritual begins with the winter solstice, when seed corn is left on the kiva altar overnight. Before the seed is planted in April or May, prayer sticks are placed at the principal springs, and prayers for rain are offered. When the farmer sets out to plant, the women in the household liberally sprinkle him and the seed with water. Then a shrine is built at the edge of the field, and corn meal and more prayers are sprinkled around it. Finally, the corn is planted, consigned to the care of earth and sky by a communicant who is aware at every possible level of the significance of the act.

Modern gardeners, in gardening organically, recover some of this reverence. In providing home ground for a diversity of animals and plants, in constructing good soil underneath our gardens, in refusing to add to the toxic load of chemicals in our environment, we contribute in a small but positive way to our battered, beleaguered planet. Religious it might not be, but reverent it certainly is.

SWEET NOURISHMENT

It's not true, as some people have said, that I garden solely to feed my compost pile. Not entirely, anyway. I do have responsibilities to all the honeybees, cabbage loopers, pipevine swallowtails, mockingbirds, praying mantises, bumblebees, paper wasps, and dragonflies I've invited into my backyard; I must keep my garden going for them, if for no other reason. And, of course, the plants I grow are beautiful and useful in themselves. There's always that. Nor must I forget to mention the obvious benefits of compost: it increases the fertility and water-holding capacity of any soil while reducing its alkalinity and susceptibility to pathogens. Yet I must admit that there's something about a compost pile that's appealing in and of itself, with or without benefits, and I can conceive of filling a garden with plants for the sole purpose of reducing them to their essence in the end.

The process could hardly be simpler. You start with kitchen scraps—melon rinds, squash innards, carrot peelings, leftover lasagna, the butt ends of cucumbers and eggplants, fingernail parings, moldy bread, cat fur, bottle corks, coffee filters, paper towels, anything organic except bones, meat, fat, and eggshells. (Bones take too long to decay, fat slows the process down, meat stinks, and, in the desert, eggshells add calcium to soils that already contain too much.) Then you pile your scraps in alternating layers with dry plant material (dead zinnias, fallen leaves) and green plant material (grass clippings, weeds), wetting each layer as you add it. Once a week or once a month you turn the pile, moving the bottom to the top, the top to the bottom and the sides to the middle. Turning aerates the contents and keeps the pile from becoming smelly and soggy. Magically, it seems, the sturdiest objects shrink, shrivel, blacken, and disappear: in a few weeks, entire grapefruits and watermelons become one with the universe, and, while corncobs and sunflower stalks linger a bit longer, they too vanish eventually, or, more accurately, become transformed into crumbly granules that smell like rich soil in a woods.

Now, when I look at potato peelings, bottle corks, and coffee grounds, I see a potential source of soil nutrients, but for years I saw only garbage, a potential source of bad odors, flies, and disease. I must have thrown away truckloads of nitrogen and phosphorus without giving it a second thought. Most of us do this every day, millions of Americans consigning incredible richness to the grinding molars of the garbage truck or the odorless security of twist-tied plastic bags: all those nutrients sealed into landfills where the soil is so lacking in oxygen that even meat won't rot, or not for years, anyway; all that nitrogen removed forever from the perpetual cycle that joins sky and earth in a mutual conspiracy of dependence and enrichment.

Most of the major nutrients cycle from sky to earth and back again like Hindu gods and their earthbound counterparts. Phosphorus, for example, spends millions of years locked up in rocks, a mere fraction of its residence time in flowers, crops, and trees. It is a relatively immobile nutrient. Where phosphate-bearing rocks are rare, the soil will lack a natural source of phosphorus. Nitrogen, on the other hand, is more readily available since it makes up nearly eighty percent of the air we breathe. However, we can't use gaseous nitrogen, and neither can plants. To be useful, nitrogen from the atmosphere must be transformed into ammonium and nitrate, simple molecules that plant roots can absorb. This work is performed by certain kinds of blue-green algae and bacteria, broadly lumped together under the rubric "nitrogen-fixers." Some nitrogen-fixers are free-living; others live inside nodules on the roots of legumes. Thanks to these microorganisms, plants take up nitrogen from the soil and incorporate it into their tissues. When a plant dies, bacteria, fungi, and protozoans release this tissue nitrogen. Some of it goes into the soil, where it may again be taken up by plants. Much becomes gaseous ammonia and returns to the atmosphere, completing the cycle.

Composting is my opportunity to participate in the endless nutrient cycles that keep our planet alive. I can do little to hasten the release of phosphorus from rocks, but my compost pile accelerates the nitrogen cycle by an order of magnitude. By keeping the pile moist and well aerated, I create the best possible conditions for the microorganisms that break down dead plant material into nitrogen and other useful nutrients. There's a regular and predictable succession of microorganisms in the pile, starting with psychrophiles, various bacteria and fungi that function best at coolish temperatures. As they digest the carbon I've supplied in the form of leaves, watermelon rinds, dead goldfish, coffee filters, and so forth, they give off heat, and the interior temperature of the pile climbs. Once it reaches seventy or ninety degrees, the psychrophilic organisms die off and actinomycetes and mesophilic bacteria take over, continuing the digestive process. They, in turn, yield to thermophilic bacteria and fungi as temperatures within the pile reach one hundred degrees and more. Eventually, the pile cools down, the microorganisms die off, and I'm left with crumbly granules of compost rich in nitrate and ammonium. The entire process takes about three months; in nature, unaided by human hands, it might require three years.

Since compost is like confidence—you can never have too much—I'm always plotting ways to increase the bulk of my pile. After exhausting the supply of fallen leaves in my own yard, I rake up leaves in city parks. On trips to the mountains, I gather bags full of pine needles and oak leaves. Once— stealthily and under cover of darkness—I filched a plastic bag of grass clippings from the university nearby. Another time, seeing a pile of cactus pads—frost-damaged discards from somebody's garden—I considered them as possible additions to my compost heap, then reluctantly abandoned the notion. With their tremendous resistance to water loss and tolerance of high temperatures, cactus pads might very well grow in a compost pile instead of rot.

No plant in my own garden is safe. At the first signs of weakness, I start to eye it covetously. The gardener in me, solicitous for its ultimate health and productivity, struggles against the composter, whose fingers itch to yank it out. My compost heap is the ultimate consolation prize. When pow- dery mildew overtook my snow peas, I bowed cheerfully to the inevitable, since I knew that their nitrogen-rich greenery would be a valuable addition to the pile. "The grim reaper," my husband called me when he saw the wheelbarrow piled high with the springy pile of peavines. He said he was afraid to nap on the couch in the evenings lest I haul him away, too.

All this came later, however. At the beginning, the art and science of composting mystified and even intimidated me. What if I did it wrong and failed? What if I did it right and failed anyway? As usual, I started with books. One assured me that, in the desert, the best gardeners were usually the best composters. It strongly implied that the best compost was made in pits. Fortunately, having recently dug a pit for an unrealized fish pond, I had one handy.

"I'm going to turn the fish pond into a compost pit," I announced to my husband at breakfast one day.

He peered over his newspaper. "The fish won't like it," he said.

I began with a layer of pyracantha leaves, raked up from under the hedge, a week's worth of kitchen scraps, and a generous dollop of blood meal, all watered thoroughly with the hose. Then I stood at the edge of the pit and peered down at my handiwork. The scant contents seemed pitifully inadequate. It would take months to fill the pit. And surely the pile shouldn't reek. All my books said that well-made compost didn't produce undesirable odors, all except for one, that is, which turned up its ladylike nose at the very idea of a compost pile. The author cited offensive odors, diseases, weeds, and plant pests as reasons why "compost bins are become more and more scarce in today's home gardens." Worse still, the author continued, *"They can breed flies!"*

As the summer passed, there was no doubt that my compost pile could and did breed flies. Cockroaches, too, several different kinds, scuttered in and out of the detritus at the bottom of the pit. Thinking of them as detritivores made me feel somewhat better, but nothing could make me feel good about flies and maggots. Don't be so middle-class, I admonished myself. If you lived in Bali, you'd be giving the local insects a week to settle into your new house before you even considered moving in. Not being Balinese, I consulted the books. Several seemed to think that putting dirt on top of the kitchen scraps would deter flies. It didn't.

Despite these and other difficulties, I persisted. I fervently believed in compost before I knew what it looked like, believed in it despite the strictures of an agriculture professor who said it would rob my soil of nitrogen. I knew it had to work because nature herself had been manufacturing and using it for millennia. Fourteen weeks after I started my first compost pile, I decided to sift its contents through half-inch mesh. The winnowed material was dark brown, moist but not wet, and granular. Not all of it was completely rotted—I could still recognize black fragments of pyracantha leaves, bits of epidermis from flower stalks, and a few melon seeds that had slipped through the mesh, but even these crumbled readily between thumb and forefinger, just like the book said.

In the end—and regardless of my anxious reading—I discovered for myself everything I needed to know. Indeed, the books misled me. The ill-inspired pit made it impossible to turn the pile and encouraged smelly, anaerobic decomposition. Sprinkling dirt atop kitchen wastes not only failed to deter flies, it inoculated the compost with innumerable small stones. Blood meal, touted as a good source of nitrogen, proved to be an unnecessary expense. Eventually, I followed my own good sense (or, more likely, the path of least resistance). I built an above-ground bin from chicken wire and spare boards. I stopped using dirt. When I added kitchen scraps, I buried them in the center of the pile where they wouldn't attract flies.

When I finally held my first compost in cupped hands—a fistful of moist, brown, crumbly granules that smelled like Old Spice cologne—it was an epiphany of sorts. "I made it," I said, then in almost the same breath realized that this was like claiming I had made my daughter. All I had done was give nature a hand.

For a while, composting became my favorite entertainment. Notoriously so, in fact, and one friend always greeted me by asking, "How's your compost pile?"

The part I love best comes after I've sifted the pile and sorted out the coarse, undigested chunks. Then, piled high in the wheelbarrow, the finished compost shivers with the motion of countless pillbugs, earwigs, and crickets. Looking down at the constantly shifting surface, I nearly swoon. My body is still but my mind feels the motion. It's like standing next to a train as it pulls away, or anchoring my toes in wet sand as retreating waves slide down the beach.

I love turning the pile, too, because this gives me a chance to inspect the process at close range. Dull brown mulberry leaves become black and slick and shiny, like obsidian. Tough stems of zucchini break down into fibrous strands. Dots of gray and orange and yellow fungi decorate leaves and bark. Sometimes thumb-sized mushrooms sprout from the perimeter of the pile. Seeds sprout, too, their ghostly white radicles blurry with root hairs, their hopeful cotyledons pressed together like praying hands. (I can't help but feel sorry for them, thwarted at the very moment when life started.) Once, as I turned the pile, an adult fig beetle, a female under the terrible compulsion to lay eggs, flung herself onto the loose compost and burrowed out of sight. I welcomed her because I knew that eventually her grubs, feeding within the pile, would help transform garbage into nitrogen, potassium, and carbon.

Sometimes rude odors arise from the pile as I peel the top layer off. Finished compost smells sweet, that's perfectly true, but compost-in-progress can smell like vomit or urine or sweaty socks or old tennis shoes or decayed teeth or dead animals. These odors, byproducts of decomposition, come from nitrogen-containing compounds with tell-tale names like *cadaverine* and *putrescine*, and they're as necessary as they are unavoidable. The stench of partly rotted garbage reminds me of what composting really involves—death and decomposition.

Middle-class fastidiousness would ordain that I find another, less odiferous, hobby. But, then, middle-class fastidiousness ordains much that is foolish, simply to spare sensibilities too long out of touch with nature's grimier side. I am as culpable as anyone. When driving on highways, I avert my eyes from the hideous corpses of mangled coyotes, cats, dogs, deer, squirrels, snakes, skunks, raccoons—the grim reaper's wasted harvest. When my cat catches birds, I cannot dispose of the dismembered bodies she leaves on the doormat, can hardly bear to walk past them when I must step out the door.

How can I touch death and come away uncontaminated? The fear lies deep, requires that we interpose cloth and wood and even metal between the dead thing and ourselves. Why else do we consign embalmed bodies to containers that are virtually impervious to moisture and mold? In this, as in many other instances, Native Americans found better ways. The Plains Indians placed their dead on high wooden platforms where ravens and vultures made quick work of what was, after all, nothing but carrion. Other peoples incinerated human remains and scattered the ashes on water or earth. This, too, rapidly recycled the nutrients in bones and organs. Less rapid but equally certain was placing the body in the soil's embrace. Even a plain pine box is an improvement over the mahogany and steel coffins that most Americans prefer. The main function of such virtually impervious containers, it seems, is to help us evade the natural cycles that make such quick work of melon vines and bean plants. We seem to be afraid to rejoin our mother, the earth. But where else did we come from in the first place? Our mothers nourished us from their own bodies, themselves nourished by the planet's fullness. We, growing up, partook freely of the earth's bounty. Why then, be so stingy at the end?

Walt Whitman, witness to the terrible slaughter of the Civil War, thought about these matters deeply, with pain and horror. "Now I am terrified at the Earth," he said. "It grows such sweet things out of such corruptions." How was it, he wondered, that he could lie down on the grass and not be contaminated by the disease and decay that had fed its flourishing blades?

The answer lies in nutrient cycles, in the transformation of one form of carbon to another. Diseases, in consuming themselves, leave nothing but basic materials. The natural cycle purifies. Ashes to ashes and dust to dust is not a threat or a dirge but a promise. Whitman understood this. The earth "gives such divine materials to men," he wrote, "and accepts such leavings from them at last."

The Mundurucu of central Brazil knew it long ago. They tell how in the old days when there were neither gardens nor cultivated plants, a young man kept pestering his old aunt for agricultural products that didn't exist. Finally, she told him to clear a patch of forest, and when he had done so, told him the names of all the crops that would grow there and how to tend, harvest, and cook them. Then she instructed him to bury her in the garden. He did as he was told, and from her body sprang all the crops of which she had spoken.

These forest-dwellers knew a truth that we find hard to accept. They understood that life springs from death and that rotting bodies are the ultimate compost. They knew, too, that from such decay sweet nourishment abounds.

GREAT EXPECTATIONS

Squashes are among the most chivalrous of plants. The male blossoms always appear first, like envoys sent to test the diplomatic climate. In zucchini, the male flower is yellow and floppy and shaped like an old-fashioned school bell. The convoluted mass of anthers inside is vaguely brainlike, as though it were the intelligence orchestrating this brave display. Each flower balances on a long, thin stalk that seems barely strong enough for the purpose, but since its burden neatly abscises after a single day, it doesn't much matter. The female flower that appears about a week later looks much the same except that it caps a pale green, pencil-thin ovary. Its stalk is sturdy and stout, well-suited to its serious purpose—a lifeline for a fruit that grows from a few ounces to a few pounds in a matter of weeks.

Meanwhile, the plants themselves explode out of the ground. Their big leaves, like umbrellas turned inside out, yearn toward the sky in the morning, then sigh earthward in the midday heat. The stocky stems creep across the ground, unable to forget that they are cucurbits, after all, hapless inheritors of vinelike tendencies. Leaves, stems, and flowers together comprise a machine designed for one purpose—mass production of zucchini fruits—and designed to do so as efficiently and quickly as possible. The plan, it would seem, involves swift build-up of leaf biomass followed by rapid increase in fruit number. More leaves mean more fruits: it's a simple exponential progression, and I gloat over the statement in a gardening book that I should check for fruit on a daily basis.

But there is, as ever, a worm in the bud, or, in this case, in the stem. I first learn about it when Tony tells me that squash vine borers, a type of moth caterpillar, sometimes live inside zucchini stems and eat the pith until the plants inexplicably wilt and collapse. "Just like that," he says and snaps his fingers. I am dubious until Barbara backs him up. She says, "One day your plants are growing great, the next day they're flattened all over the ground." Squashed, in fact.

At first, mine seem fine. A mysterious yellow substance like cornmeal trickles out of the stems, but I think nothing of it. Proudly, I pick the first fruits of my garden, a total of four zucchini, in late May. Three are a respectable size, about six inches long or so. The fourth isn't really a keeper. I keep it anyway, and spend my evenings leafing through cookbooks. In sheer desperation, it seems, many cooks toss handfuls of zucchini more or less at random into any kind of stew or casserole. I hope to do better, and, with my mouth watering slightly, I mark recipes for zucchini bread, zucchini muffins, zucchini relish, zucchini marmalade, zucchini pancakes, fried zucchini, stuffed zucchini, zucchini tempura, and zucchini quiche.

At about this point, hubris receives the required comeuppance. The leaves of my zucchini plants droop and develop yellow blotches. Fruit production falls to almost nothing. It's the heat, I say at first; then, turning to an old horticulture textbook, I convince myself that my zucchini plants have wilt, a bacterial disease for which there is no cure. Eating the delicately flavored fruits as I contemplate their doom becomes a bittersweet experience, like spending a perfect day with a lover before he leaves for the front. Meanwhile, cornmeal dribbles from the stems.

Why the zucchini? I moan. Why not the Armenian cucumbers? These, the only cucumbers that do well in our climate, are madly successful, but I don't much like their flavor, an insipid, almost dusty taste nothing like the crisp, assertive tang of a really good cucumber. I sneer at my former solicitude for the young vines: weaving each succulent shoot in and out of the chicken-wire trellis, I took all possible care lest I break or injure even one, so precious did they seem. Now, having buried the wire under a mass of stem and leaf, they fling wild shoots into the air as if seeking to corral unwary passersby. Miles of vine twine in and out of the chicken wire. I can hardly believe that so much biomass comes from an annual root.

All this is amazing and gratifying in itself, but it isn't until the vines start fruiting that I truly understand what I've done to myself. Cucumber vines have no sense of proportion, I discover then: overcome with their own largess, they would as soon produce a thousand fruits as ten. My delight at the first four or five tiny cucumbers the size of my little finger turns to dismay as those four or five are succeeded by eight or ten, and those eight or ten by fifty or sixty. Suddenly I confront a host of cucumbers ripening at once. Any that I miss—and it's easy to overlook them in the verdure—eventually loom into view, pregnant with reproach and mesoderm.

This is success beyond my wildest dreams. I have, in fact, transcended mere success and ventured into some new dimension where hypersuccess mocks my modest intentions. Three meals a day are not enough to keep up with the productivity of my vines. My husband and I eat cucumbers sliced raw into salads, marinated in oil and vinegar, stuffed with tuna, drenched in yogurt or sour cream, seasoned with dill, with tarragon, with mint, with rosemary. Poring over cookbooks, I find myself strangely attracted to recipes I'd laughed at before, recipes for cucumber soup, cucumber curry, even fried cucumbers. I try every single one and still have more cucumbers than I can use because they keep on coming like widgets on a conveyer belt.

The queen of cucumbers, I give them away with a generous hand and a large smile. When no one will accept any more, I begin slicing them into the kitchen wastebasket, guiltily at first, then with something approaching malicious glee. Finally, I consign them directly to the compost bin. I don't even bother with the charade of bringing them indoors and refrigerating them for a day or two first.

I read hopefully about fatal diseases of cucumbers in my gardening books. There seems to be any number of possibilities, including blight, wilt, and stunt. (Obviously, it's too late for stunt.) Every five minutes in these United States of America, another cucumber vine succumbs to wilt, so why not in my backyard? But my vines, bursting with impudent good health, thrive despite me.

The zucchini, however, look worse and worse. If they were Catholic, I'd summon a priest. Then comprehension descends. The cornmeal, the wilting, the loss of production: there's only one possible explanation. Grabbing a kitchen knife, I rush into the garden, slit one stem, pull it open to reveal a plump, black-snouted grub. A squash vine borer, of course. The cornmeal is its frass, and the daily wilting results from loss of water-conducting tissue as the grub nibbles at the pith. All my zucchini plants are afflicted. One stem, a kind of borer condominium, harbors three grubs stacked one above the other. I have two alternatives, both equally unacceptable: to pull out all the plants now (and save on water bills) or to let them die a lingering death (and harvest a few last zucchini). I choose the former to spare myself emotional wear and tear.

There's no lack of that for desert gardeners, anyway. All summer long my garden pins medals on me with one hand and administers slaps with the other. I brag about my thirty-five-pound watermelons which are so wet and sweet I rejoice in having lived long enough to taste them. On the other hand, the eggplants refuse to grow. Only one of six sets any fruit at all, and these remain stubbornly hard and fist-sized. Hanging on the plants like small, purple hand grenades, they announce my incompetence to the world at large. The first six ears of corn are the best I've ever eaten in my entire life. "I could happily die right now," I tell my husband as we polish them off. The following six, thoroughly riddled with earworms, are fit only for the compost pile. In the next thunderstorm, all the cornstalks fall over (*lodging* is what farmers call it, my husband tells me helpfully). My entire crop consisted of twelve ears, half inedible.

It is always this way with gardening. Mad success and impotent failure mingle so thoroughly that the bewildered gardener hardly knows whether to glow with pride or cover her face in shame. This is hard to take, since I prefer my dilemmas to be clear-cut. But the garden seems to hint that success and failure are not immiscible opposites like oil and water. Maybe they are more like sediment suspended in water, a colloidal mixture in which the individual granules are indistinguishable until they have settled to the bottom of the glass. And that might take a long time.

Gardening is difficult no matter where you are, Henry Mitchell pointed out. He was thinking mainly of the occasional natural disasters—floods, tornadoes, hurricanes—that rip apart a decade of nurturing in a matter of hours or even minutes. In the desert, where every summer day is a natural disaster of sorts, the difficulty of gardening verges on impossibility.

Knowing what to expect makes endurance no easier. It's so hot most days that laundry on the clothesline dries before the next load stops spinning in the washing machine. At midday even the deeply rooted shade trees droop. They can't take up water fast enough to counteract the desiccating heat. Mature zucchini leaves sag, and the youngest ones wither and blacken unless the soil is quite wet. Indoors we make ourselves as comfortable as possible with air conditioning or evaporative cooling, but outdoors we are at the desert's mercy, and when the temperature climbs above one hundred and ten degrees for the third day in a row, we step outside only long enough to twist the faucet that delivers life-saving liquid to our gardens.

The Tohono O'odham, Native Americans who have lived and farmed in this desert for centuries, have learned that summer gardening in the desert is a matter of training your expectations to the possible. They work with the natural rhythm of summer instead of struggling against it. They plant their summer gardens near the end of June just before the rains begin. Their crops—tepary beans, corn, squash, chile—have been selected to grow and fruit in the short space of time when water is relatively plentiful. I could follow their example, but I don't. Their corn is for grinding, not eating off the cob. Their beans, a kind of pinto, are harvested when dry. Their squash are winter squash, meant for storage. No zucchini, no string beans, no sweet corn. Only their melons promise flavors that can't be saved but must be savored at once or not at all.

And so I struggle to grow vegetables and flowers bred for milder climates. Is it failure when I don't succeed? Or does failure lie in setting an impossible task in the first place?

Either way, the end of summer finds my garden (and me)

in disarray. We are routed troops, ashamed, disaffected, without an ounce of fight left in us. The garden seems a burden, as importunate as an infant, incessant in its requirements. Water me, harvest me, trim me, it begs. But no matter how much water I pour onto the vegetables, they still suffer—tomato leaves leathery and curled, cucumber leaves bronzed and cracked. A plant physiologist tries to console me: "Heat like this is beyond the physiological tolerance of most vegetables," he says. "They're not cacti, after all." (Your typical cactus can withstand temperatures up to 145 degrees Fahrenheit once it has been properly acclimated.)

The flowers look as tatty as bag ladies—overgrown, leggy, sagging away from their stakes, dusty from powdery mildew. By picking deadheads, I've prolonged their lives unnaturally, and they resent it. Watermelons split just before they ripen, then attract a diverse assembly of ants, beetles, fungi, and bacteria. Cantaloupes, scalded by the sun and not worth picking, rot in place. Leaf-footed bugs beset the tomatoes. Inserting their proboscises into the skin, they inject bacteria that cause the fruits to spoil right on the vine. Small green grasshoppers gnaw at the few tomatoes that escape the leaf-footed bugs. I yearn to respond with massive doses of insecticide, but I'm an organic gardener. My hands are tied. Surveying the damage, I decide that the garden reached its peak in June. Now, in August, it looks exhausted—too much sun, too much heat, too much fecundity.

I don't invite anyone to see my garden when it looks like this. In our society, the twin poles of success and failure have taken the place of conventional morality. Success equals moral triumph while failure at anything signals moral decay, and I want no one to think I'm morally deficient.

At the end of every summer, when the decline and disarray of August weigh upon me, it takes an effort of will to return to gardening. Neglect has fed upon itself as it does in keeping a diary. While a diary can be set aside temporarily, a garden can't estivate in a drawer. Especially in the desert, it requires some level of attention, no matter how you feel. Gardens are a discipline and a responsibility, then, as well as a pleasure, and it is my sense of responsibility that sends me into the garden at last. As I reclaim the gravel paths from sprawling tomato vines, I alternate between feelings of accomplishment and guilt. It's good to be getting the mess cleaned up at last, but my conscience pricks me when I notice that the vines I had thought were half dead are really half alive. Fresh green leaves unfold at the stem tips and hopeful flowers open here and there. A few have even set small, hard fruits. Reeling with the fruity scent of overripe cantaloupe and the stench of rotting pulp, I rake up the tangle of half-dead melon vines. When I drop a cantaloupe by accident, it collapses with a slurpy sigh. Three wheelbarrow-loads of melon vine go directly into the compost bin. I yank out the beans, too; not until I've cleared away half the row do I notice that some have produced new, dark green, velvety leaves in response to the last summer storm.

As I work, I think about success and failure in the garden and elsewhere. How quickly the successes fade. How long the failures linger. Strange that the former seem ascribable as much to luck as skill while the latter seem to be no one's fault but my own. The heartbreaking failure of my zucchini overshadowed my stunning success with Armenian cucumbers, made it seem like an aberration. I discount the successes, exaggerate the failures because that's the way I am. I fight with my garden the same way I fight with myself, alternately exhorting it to greater effort and giving up in despair. My garden, I observe not for the first time, is a microcosm of myself. Or am I a microcosm of it?

Piling tomato vines into the wheelbarrow, I remember one particular September, one richer than usual in end-of-the-summer discouragements. I wasn't even certain that I would have a winter garden. I'd made the necessary preparations out of discipline, not desire: taken down the straggling lengths of string that once made a neat, taut border around the vegetable bed; coiled each strand into a tidy quoit and set it aside; pulled up the stakes that had anchored the string. Then I turned on the soaker hose, more for the soil's sake than for any other reason, because the earth needed nourishment and care. And that's when I knew I would have a winter garden. I needed nourishment and care myself. What better source than my garden?

RIPENESS IS ALL

"Sow radishes when daffodils bloom," suggests one of my seed catalogs. "Bunching onions should be seeded when your crocuses are finally in full bloom. Summer squash and cucumber germinate better if you wait 'til the roses bloom." Supposedly, it's all part of nature's own gardening calendar, a foolproof guide to sowing seeds. Unless, of course, you live in the desert, in which case much traditional gardening wisdom comes aslant, the way a stake immersed in water appears bent at a peculiar angle.

What use can I possibly make of the suggestion that I accumulate kitchen scraps in big plastic bags all winter long, setting them on the back porch where they'll stay frozen until spring? What good are the fancy, long-season hybrids when my growing seasons won't accommodate them? Here, where daffodils and crocuses are as rare as rain in June, we sow our radishes and bunching onions in the fall, around the time we might be setting out daffodil bulbs themselves. By the first day of spring, seedlings of zucchini, cucumber, watermelon, basil, and snap bean should already be popping out of the ground, and if our summer squashes and cucumbers aren't blooming a month before the first roses, we've been laggardly indeed.

Gardening imparts a sense of place and time that little else can. The Algonquin Indians of Massachusetts knew that the flowering of red maple alone wasn't a reliable indicator for corn planting. Only when oak and dogwood joined the maple and the whippoorwill and catbird began to call would the soil be warm enough for corn to germinate. The desert gardener must be wise enough to prepare her own calendar. She starts tomato seeds on a windowsill or under grow-lights in January when the house finches and Anna's hummingbirds start to sing. She sows seeds of summer crops about the time that prickly pears sprout soft, new pads, usually in the middle of March, or she can wait until the harvester ants begin to stir in April, a sure sign that the soil is now warm. Once the mesquite leafs out, all danger of frost is assuredly past, and she can move tender potted plants outdoors.

Now, of course, we can use thermometers to track the springtime warming of earth and air. In times past, though, gardeners and farmers necessarily relied on natural events like leaf budding as an assay of environmental changes. They understood that wild plants are tuned to signals so faint that human senses can't detect them. In the seasonally dry tropics of Costa Rica, for instance, many trees flower in response to a complicated combination of day length and rainfall. Flower buds begin to develop as nights lengthen, then remain in an embryonic state until the rains start, whereupon development quickly resumes and the entire forest bursts into bloom at once.

In the temperate zone, temperature takes precedence over rainfall in determining flowering time. Certain ornamental cherry trees, for example, can't initiate flower buds when the air temperature is below forty-two degrees. Moreover, be-

fore they can complete flower development, the air temperature must have been forty-two degrees or higher for a total
of forty-eight hundred hours. (It takes longer to achieve this
temperature sum in a cold spring than in a warm one, which
is why the date of first flowering varies from year to year.)

In any zone, torrid or temperate, flowering, fruiting, and
leafing must be timed to happen at the perfect moment. It
does a plant no good to flower just before the first frost
withers its stems or to fruit at the beginning of the dry season
when its seeds, unable to germinate, will be eaten by ants and
rodents.

Although wild plants respond predictably to environmental signals, gardeners can't always rely on them for planting
cues. The Navajo say that if the cliff rose blooms in October,
the winter will be snowy. But cliff rose flowers in response
to rain. A heavy shower in September will almost certainly
bring cliff rose into bloom in October. Plants know only the
past, not the future. Phenology is at best a rough guide to
planting and can't protect the gardener against extraordinary
events, like the April snowfall that knocked all the blossoms
off my peach tree one year.

I wonder if we are less wise now that we have thermometers and hygrometers and dozens more devices with which
to measure our environment. The thermometer that tells us
when corn should go into the ground also lets us ignore the
subtle phenology of the natural world. I like to think of that
Algonquin farmer standing at the edge of woods, watching
quietly for the silent shift from winter into spring, and I'd be
sorry to hear that now he sat at a computer terminal instead.
Data should never pass for wisdom.

So, unfairly ignored by garden books and seed catalogs, I
turn to gardening friends for advice and consolation. Draw-

ing upon their knowledge, I reap the cumulative wisdom of fifty years. Ed tells me in June that it's not too late to start corn. His always grows well under drip irrigation, he says. Toni confesses that she doesn't dig up her garden at the end of the summer; she just squeezes in compost and winter crops wherever she can find the space. Richard advises me to heap dirt or sand around the base of zucchini and cucumber plants to deter squash borers. Bob thinks that a collar of aluminum foil around the stems is more effective. Tony advocates stove ashes. Nancy covers her zucchini plants with netting, and then, to discourage the bees as well as the borers, she pollinates the flowers by hand. Barbara says she sets out her tomato plants in the middle of February. Sometimes frost gets them, but if it doesn't, she'll be harvesting her first tomatoes a month before the rest of us. Toni mentions that she never bothers to plant tomatoes anymore; she gets all the fruit she needs from volunteers. "Just throw an overripe tomato onto the ground and all the seeds will come up," she says.

I try all this and more. To keep squash-vine borers from laying eggs on my zucchini plants, I paint some stems with fingernail polish and daub others with Tanglefoot, a sticky concoction that mires any insect unfortunate enough to touch it. I plant rows of bush peas back to back so that they'll support one another and save me the trouble of erecting a more formal trellis. I start my tomato seeds in pure compost and plant a hedge of sunflowers to shade the mature tomato plants. Some of this works, some of it doesn't. The bush peas, a luxuriant tangle of leaf and tendril and pod, thrive, but nothing deters the borers, and the summer is so hot that the sunflower hedge itself could use some shade. Soon I'm passing on advice of my own. "Don't worry about the wasps," I tell Toni. "Some kinds eat caterpillars, you know. That's why I never have a problem with tomato hornworms." In another six months, as we talk about gardening, she will inform me that wasps prey upon caterpillars. "Somebody told me that," she will say, "I don't remember who."

Despite all their accumulated experience, none of my gardening friends can answer my most pressing questions or solve my most heartbreaking problems. Why do my tomatoes crack? Why do so many marble-sized fruits drop from my watermelon vines? And what is an absolutely reliable, totally foolproof way of telling when the melons are ripe?

"You can't grow watermelons here," is all the advice they have, but it's too late. Somehow, against the odds and contrary to the books, I have succeeded in doing so, and now I need more immediate help. My mother, who grew up on a Texas truck farm, says that her father waited to pick until the underside of the melons turned yellow. The books disagree with one another. One author reports that unripe melons give off a metallic or ringing sound when thumped, while ripe melons produce a more muffled response. Steel drum versus timpani is how I imagine it. (My brother-in-law advises me to tap my head. "That's the sound you want," he says.) Another book insists that an unripe melon says "Think," while a ripe one says "Thump." Mine evidently don't speak the same language as his, for all reverberate to the same monotonous note, neither steel drum nor timpani, but the uninformative plunk of a dowel on a block of wood.

Impatience makes the decision for me, and I begin the great annual tradition of harvesting the first watermelon much too early. Every year, as soon as I plunge the knife into the rind, my heart sinks, for the flesh resists the blade. Sure enough, when the two halves of the melon separate, they reveal soft, white seeds embedded in pale, pulpy flesh. I should grow only cantaloupes, which present no such dilemmas. When ripe, the muskmelon type roll right off the vine, revealing a sticky, round umbilicus that exudes enough fragrance to perfume a stable. All I need do is brush off the little sugar ants that collect its sweetness drop by drop. Sometimes, rummaging among the criss-crossing vines, I locate ripe cantaloupes by smell alone, just like the ants themselves.

Ripeness is all, says a son to his father in *King Lear*. By ripeness, he means perfect readiness to act or to endure, whichever seems best. For the gardener, too, ripeness is all, since it culminates months of labor and gallons of water—many gallons in the case of a watermelon. At first, the zygote—the new individual created when egg and sperm fuse—remains quite small as it undergoes rapid cell division. Once the necessary number of cells have been produced, the fruit begins to swell. As individual cells stretch to three hundred thousand times their original size, the shape of the fruit changes to accommodate them, and in forty days or so it balloons from an ovary the size of a garbanzo bean to a twenty-six-pound behemoth.

This explosion in growth represents a tremendous mobilization of resources, the sole purpose of which is to concentrate sugar within the fruit. The process is strictly regulated by hormones. An embryonic tomato, for instance, can be brought to maturity in a laboratory petri dish by injection of the proper hormones in the correct sequence. In melons, hormones engineer the requisition of nutrients and photosynthate from nearby leaves or even at the expense of distant stems and leaves if necessary. Flower buds and blossoms may be sacrificed as well, since the existing leaves won't be able to support them. It's no wonder that many fruits never develop beyond the size of a pea. A given volume of vine is capable of maturing only a limited number of fruits, so the excess must be aborted. The alternative would be a crop of melons no bigger than golf balls and perhaps about as sweet.

Sweetness, after all, is the whole point. It's the sugar that lures us to the vine, the sugar that enlists us as deliberate or inadvertent dispersers of the seeds. That tremendous mobilization of resources was aimed at creating exactly this conjunction between consumer and consumed, disperser and dispersed. It is aimed, moreover, to keep it from happening too soon. The conjunction must occur at the moment of perfect readiness.

So ripeness is all, and judging it is a skill that can be learned. I finally learned that watermelons are ripe when the tendrils nearest the fruit wither from soft, green curlicues to hard, brown prongs. At this point, hormone production slows or stops, and enlargement also ceases. The melon is ripe and ready to be picked; if left on the vine it will only deteriorate.

From seed to vine to melon to seed, the cycle repeats itself summer after summer. Because the seed is consumed in the process, the end point is never exactly the same as the starting point. The cycle is imperfect, and so it is in human lives. We enter the world as infants and exit it as old men and women: this is our phenology. While the seasons cycle within our lives, we ourselves follow a different trajectory. We travel a line from birth to death, yet, so strong is the impact of natural cycles all around us, and so hopeful are we that death is not the end, that we devise complicated philosophical systems to prove that aging belongs to a cycle, that death is not the closing but the opening of a door.

I wish I could believe it myself. Now perched on the edge of forty, I might be halfway through my life, and the knowledge distresses me unduly. When I hold my hand just so, the skin on the back of my wrist looks as frail as tissue paper. I'm half-afraid that if I raise my palm to the light, it will be translucent, my bones visible as though seen through X-rays. It saddens me, this sign of aging, more so than the gray hairs that have become too numerous to pluck, because it indicates a loss of elasticity in my skin and perhaps in other ways, as well. Aging may turn out to be a process in which I become less resilient to misfortune and my mind springs less readily to perform expected tasks.

I am pilgrim on the road to age and, needing guideposts and way-stations, I covertly observe my grandmother, now ninety-two. I watch her shuffle, cane in hand, from one room to the next, give her my arm on uneven sidewalks, boost her by the elbows when her joints have stiffened from sitting. For long periods she sits silently, tatting a chain of lace or, more often these days, simply doing nothing. She tends to drift into sleep at such times, as though the passageway between waking and sleeping has become widened with age so that the brain's tide slips freely back and forth between the two. Watching her, I can easily imagine that death comes gradually as increasing sleepiness until finally the eyes never open from that last, tempting doze.

Is this what frightens us most about aging—the approach of death? Or is it the opportunities lost, never to be recaptured, the deeds postponed, never to be achieved? I remember turning twenty-one and complaining that I was no longer young; the middle-aged people to whom I confided my plight were legitimately peeved. To them I was a millionaire mourning the loss of a five-dollar bill. Then, I witnessed their irritation without understanding it. Now, I comprehend that I had most of my life before me while theirs was more than half used up.

At twenty-one, life is still as fragrant with possibilities as a cantaloupe is with sweetness: for all anyone knows, we truly will turn out to be another Curie, Darwin, Vivaldi, van Gogh. But at forty-five, this is no longer so. If at forty, fifty, sixty, we have not made our first million, pitched a no-hitter, traveled to the source of the White Nile, written words that will last as long as the Bible, the chances that we will yet do so become increasingly small. In all likelihood we have reached the height of our powers.

Distressed to see what a puny height it is, we find it difficult to stifle regrets for years wasted, especially all the time
spent idly, destructively, stupidly. Those thousands of hours
spent working crossword puzzles, nursing hangovers, watching television, reading romance novels, loitering in shopping
malls—what might I have accomplished had I spent them instead at the cello, the microscope, the computer? That decade
when everyone but me was in graduate school and I could
see no further into the future than my next romance—what
wouldn't I give to have those years back again? As I review
the choices I made and see how I unfailingly picked the easier
alternative every time, I want to return and follow a more
challenging route.

Aging in humans, as ripening in melons, is under hor-
monal and genetic control; that we will age, and will do
so according to pattern, is inevitable—but ripeness is not.
Old age does not necessarily bring greater wisdom, accep-
tance, humility. Sometimes it brings only bitterness or regrets. Often its physical infirmities swamp the emotional
and mental graces acquired with such effort. I can only hope
(without much assurance of success) that I am closing in on
ripeness as I age. Sometimes I actually think now before I
speak. Is this ripeness, I wonder? I take care lest I unintentionally speak a wounding truth or inadvertently blurt out
secrets that aren't mine to tell. Surely this counts as a kind
of wisdom. I, who have always despised philosophy as the
useless recreation of idle men, now enter into unilateral, lop-
sided battles with Socrates, Plato, Milton. I take up gardening, always associated in my mind with doddering oldsters,
and am surprised to find it requires ample strength of mind
and body.

Forty-six days after the first watermelon blossoms appear,
my husband announces that, in his opinion, the largest melon
is now ripe. "Why don't you plug it?" he suggests. With some

trepidation, I repair to the melon patch with a sharp knife and a roll of duct tape. If the melon isn't ripe, I reason, I can re-insert the plug and tape up the wound so as not to attract ants. This proves unnecessary. The plug is sweet and succulent and pink and black-seeded and warm. This melon, at least, has achieved its goal in life. We each take a nibble, then I cut the umbilicus and hoist the melon out of the tangle of vines.

It's said that you can do everything right and still fail to harvest a worthwhile crop of watermelons. Somehow, I did everything wrong and succeeded anyway. Who is to say that making all the wrong choices doesn't lead as surely to ripe-ness as making all the right ones? Given time enough to ripen, we can make peace with even our worst failures and short-comings. Given time enough to ripen, we can find that even death loses its terror.

The Algonquin watches for oak blossom and listens for catbird song before he plants. The desert-dwelling Tohono O'odham waits for the fruiting of saguaros. Each follows the inherent wisdom of his time and place. In the end we each must find our own wisdom. This exploratory process seems to be what human lives are best suited for, and most of us need every one of our allotted twenty-six thousand days if we are to bring ourselves to anything like ripeness.

Ordinary Miracles

Spring, rainbows,

ordinary miracles

about which

nothing new can be said.

ERICA JONG

A FULL LIFE IN A SMALL PLACE

A soft buzz at my elbow announces the arrival of a leaf-cutter bee. Slightly smaller than a honeybee, she is banded with white and black her entire length. She lands on the edge of a lilac leaf, then scissors out a circlet of tissue, clinging to the cut portion as she works, a lumberjack standing on the wrong end of a limb. With the last snip she saws off the limb and drops into thin air, then zips away, holding the circlet, now rolled into a tube, beneath her.

At that moment, a western kingbird—a flash of yellow belly and black tail—somersaults off the telephone wires overhead. I'm afraid he'll catch my bee, but he loops after a sputtering cicada instead, snaps it out of the sky and returns to his perch. There he bangs the bug against the wire, flips it in the air a few times and finally gulps it down.

As I start to record the bee and the bird in my garden journal, a pair of black-chinned hummingbirds grabs my attention. The female hangs in mid-air like a crescent moon as the male spirals high above her, then plummets, wind bleating in his tail feathers, and sweeps upward again. For a moment he hangs invisible against the sun, then he dives back into visibility, a metallic green bomber, a hurtling, ounce-sized package of feathers and lust.

Nearby, two giant swallowtails are putting on a similar performance. The female, a large, yellow and black butterfly missing one of her commalike tails, feeds nonchalantly at one zinnia blossom after another. She coils and uncoils her capillary tongue in and out of the tiny florets as though she had nothing else in the world to do. Meanwhile, the male hovers frantically behind, beside and sometimes before her, never stopping to rest or feed. His body is nearly vertical, and his rapidly beating wings are spread wide like a duck about to land on water. Suddenly, losing all patience he rushes at her, and they spurt upwards, beating against one another. I can hear their wings brush together. Then they float over the hedge and out of sight.

As I pick up my journal, I glimpse the cat crouched among the herbs, lashing her tail. Hurrying over, I see her bat cautiously at a newly emerged butterfly, an orange fritillary with silver-spangled wings. Its chrysalis, a tattered husk as frail as a dried leaf, hangs empty on a nearby twig. The butterfly huddles, wings folded, in the protection of the rosemary bush. I grab the cat and we watch together. Has she already damaged it? No. The fritillary opens and closes its wings a few times, then laboriously crawls up the leafy staircase to the topmost stem, where it opens its wings one more time, then glides like a paper airplane to the flower patch six feet away.

I toss my journal aside. Obviously, this is a day for living, not recording life. How amazing that first flight is. One second the butterfly is completely new and untried, then with a single downbeat it becomes airborne, floating on tissue paper wings with instant expertise. As Erica Jong says, it is no less a miracle for being ordinary.

In fact, the entire morning has been a congeries of miracles, and I hardly know which amazes me most—the swallowtail's humble perseverance or the hummingbird's flamboyant acrobatics, the bee's mechanical actions or the kingbird's dazzling improvisations. And to think that I saw it on Mulberry Street, as Dr. Seuss writes. To think it all happened in my own backyard.

Merely in planting a few vegetables and flowers, I have set in motion an entire ecosystem. Bumblebees, carpenter bees, honeybees, leaf-cutter bees, as many kinds of wasps, gulf fritillaries, pipevine swallowtails, giant swallowtails, mockingbirds, kingbirds, hummingbirds, and on and on— all these enliven the garden and even depend on it for sustenance. Their abundance shows what a cornucopia the city is during these early summer months when the desert is empty-handed. While cabbage whites, giant swallowtails, painted ladies, and pipevine swallowtails jostle one another in urban gardens, there's not a butterfly to be seen beyond the city limits.

Over the few years of my garden's existence, I've kept an informal tally of organisms seen there. Every time a new bird or butterfly makes even the briefest appearance, I rush outside with field guide and binoculars. So far, I've counted twenty-three species of butterflies, thirty-four of birds and three of lizards, not to mention hundreds of insects that will, unfortunately, remain forever anonymous since I can't do much more than categorize them by order, suborder and, sometimes, family: beetles, true bugs, leafhoppers, grasshoppers, flies, aphids, wasps, bees, ants, damselflies, dragonflies, moths, and so forth. Some I know to genus by their activities: the bee that cuts my lilac leaves is, perforce, a leaf-cutter bee and belongs to the genus *Megachile*; same with the leaf-cutting ants—genus *Acromyrmex*—that collect leaves and flower petals from all over the yard. A few are so distinctive I can call them by name: the green fig beetle that piles up in windrows after summer rains, the obnoxious black cactus beetle that gnaws the pads of my prickly pear, the rather terrifying staghorn beetle, a cross between a lobster and a rhinoceros, that comes to lights in the summertime. But most are simply Grasshopper or Katydid or Damselfly, as though my garden were some children's book come to life.

If I were willing to kill my insect visitors and residents and submit them to identification by a proper entomologist, I'd have an extremely large figure to report, no doubt. Many years ago, an entomologist who lived in the suburbs of New York City did just this and found over fourteen hundred species of insects in his yard. Four hundred sixty-seven of these were butterflies and moths (mostly moths). Flies and beetles ran neck-and-neck at two hundred fifty-eight and two hundred fifty-nine species apiece. He collected seventy-five species of Homoptera, mostly aphids of one sort or another.

But I prefer not to employ a killing jar in what is, after all, a pesticide-free zone. If I capture and poison each solitary insect as I see it—the orange dragonfly that perches over the fish pond on hot summer afternoons, the lone mountain emperor butterfly that nectars at fallen dates—what will be left of my garden's diversity? The arch predator in my garden—Katie, my tortoiseshell cat—has already made considerable inroads in the numbers and diversity of the lizard population, and the mouse she brought for my inspection was the only one I've ever seen in my yard. I'd say one top carnivore per garden is enough. More interesting and less destructive is speculation about why this small space should be home to such a variety of living creatures.

One reason is that, even in the middle of the city, the desert around us makes itself known. City and desert are not, after all, mutually incompatible entities like the positive poles of two different magnets. Instead of repelling one another, they interact in unpredictable and interesting ways. The perimeter of the city is also a zone of contact with the desert, the coarsest in a series of screens that becomes successively finer towards the center. An enormous variety of creatures can pass through the outermost screen, and people who live on the city's edge coexist with animals that I'll never see in my garden: javelinas (wild pigs that root for bulbs and roots); jackrabbits, perennially thirsty and apt to nibble any green, growing shoot left unprotected by a wall or fence; coyotes, quick to learn which households are a soft touch for water and food scraps; rodents of many sorts and a variety of snakes to prey upon them; and the richest possible array of birds, from vermilion flycatchers in low-lying mesquite forests to whispering flocks of black-throated sparrows on higher, more arid ground.

Few, if any, of these creatures pass through the series of screens to the city center where confirmed urbanites like pigeons and English sparrows scrounge a living on sidewalks and parking lots. But between the outermost ring and the central core is a wide zone of ordinary neighborhoods, a mosaic of houses, little parks, shopping centers, gardens, ravines, trees, lawns, and vacant lots where a number of desert animals find habitat that suits their needs. These are, for the most part, not the wildest, rarest creatures; they are, rather, the ones that can coexist with human ways, like horned lizards or mockingbirds, or that can live on such a small scale they generally escape detection, like pillbugs or ants. My garden supports many such.

City gardeners unintentionally entice certain animals into town by cultivating small deserts in their own front yards. Even a lone paloverde or a single saguaro can be an island of desert. Multiply this by hundreds of yards across the city, and you have an archipelago of wild and half-wild places. On almost every island in the archipelago, no matter how small, you can find some creature that belongs to the desert—in the spring, giant mesquite bugs, vividly painted like African masks, cling to new pods and fresh green growth of mesquite trees, and all year long, Gila woodpeckers, raucous birds with houndstooth backs and red caps, treat saguaros as oversized birdhouses. In this way, the desert imprints itself on the city, another reminder of who we are and where we live.

There is more to my garden's diversity than proximity to the desert. In the garden world, as in the great world outside, diversity of animal life depends on diversity of niches, a niche being the sum of everything an animal does (eating, mating, hibernating) and requires (food, mates, burrows). My garden, a place of shade trees, thorny hedges, bare earth, and flowery patches, provides space and material for any number of creatures.

The leaf-cutter bee, for example, needs flowers for nectar, leaves for nesting materials, and someplace to construct her nests. My sunflowers provide the first, my lilac and passion-flower supply the second, and the frame of my kitchen window serves as the third. The damselfly niche centers around water, and my fish pond, tiny as it is, gives half a dozen damselflies room enough for feeding, sparring, mating, and laying eggs. Mockingbirds, constant carolers from telephone poles and treetops, need high perches for singing and display-ing, an abundance of ground-dwelling insects, and dense foli-age for nests. My garden provides all three, and a mocking-bird pair has resided here for years.

Partitioning of resources allows many more species to co-exist than if all ate exactly the same things. Curve-billed thrashers, for instance, feed on the same ground-dwelling insects as mockingbirds, but they also dig beneath the sur-face for grubs, while mockingbirds do not. By partitioning the food resource in my garden, thrashers and mockingbirds create separate niches for themselves. Some creatures, particularly insects, are master partitioners, feeding specialists that eat only one thing. Giant mesquite bugs, for example, suck juices from the cell walls of mesquite pods and twigs. That's all they consume, and without the mesquite tree in my garden, I would have no mesquite bugs. Hornworms require tomato plants, and skeletonizers require grapevines. By diversifying my plantings, I increase the diversity of animals in my garden.

Diversity begets yet more diversity, literally feeding on itself, a result of the simple principle that anything in the living world can consider itself edible. Every carbon-based life-form, from a splinter of wood to a human blood cell, can provide food for some other life-form. Pollen, nectar, excrement, flesh: it's all grist for the mill. Aphids feed on my broccoli, ants milk the aphids, and horned lizards snap up the ants. Fallen leaves, when left on the ground, are the basis of another food chain, starting with detritivores like earwigs, cockroaches, pillbugs, and snails, and ending with birds like curve-billed thrashers and cactus wrens. Wild pipevine in the alley provides food for pipevine caterpillars, which, in turn, become food for the paper wasps that tirelessly cruise the garden all day long, which become food for the western king-birds that perch on the phone lines overhead. Cabbage white caterpillars feed on the broccoli leaves, warblers feed on the cabbage white caterpillars, and Katie the cat, unfortunately, feeds on the warblers.

Many of these simple food chains merge to form complex food webs. The larvae of butterflies and moths are, in fact, the basis for a major food web in my garden, since a variety of species, especially ichneumon wasps and tachinid flies, prey upon them all summer long. Aphids, abundant during the winter and spring, would be a major nuisance but for the variety of predators they attract—obvious ones like verdins, sparrows and warblers as well as more cryptic ones like the larvae of lacewings, ladybugs and syrphid flies. Since these insects have predators of their own—praying mantises, assassin bugs, robber flies, and so forth—aphids are the basis for a second major food web. The amazing thing is not that my garden is so rich in species; it's that there's any room left for me.

On any given day I might, as certain visitors have, step outside, survey my garden, and say, "There's nothing going on here," but the cumulative total of garden creatures suggests that on many other days there is. Time eventually gives me the variety I might otherwise achieve by size. After all, if you sit in one place long enough, the entire landscape changes— oceans wash over farmland and retreat, leaving a layer cake of limestone sediments, glaciers scoop out valleys and basins as easily as your thumb imprints damp clay.

Watching my garden across the year, I see how time adds and subtracts diversity. Migrating birds briefly augment the avian population according to season. White-crowned sparrows, song sparrows, green-tailed towhees, yellow-rumped warblers, orange-crowned warblers, Wilson's warblers, black-throated gray warblers—all these visit early in the spring on their way north. In the autumn, rufous hummingbirds, en route from Alaska to southern Mexico, the longest migrational flight of any North American hummingbird, create havoc at my feeders in their desperate need for energy. Desert birds like phainopeplas and pyrrholoxias appear briefly in the arid months of May and June. They would rather stay in the desert, I think, but hunger drives them to seek food wherever it can be found, and in dry years, city gardens are a resource they dare not ignore. Insects, too, are bound to time, or at least to its seasonal manifestations. Winters are relatively quiet—nothing much but aphids and a few cabbage whites, those delicate white butterflies whose slender green caterpillars devour my broccoli and chard. Once summer rains begin, there's a dramatic surge in insect populations as dragonflies, green fig beetles, cloudless sulphurs, grasshoppers, and many others materialize from wherever they've waited out the dry season.

In this way, the population of my garden rises and falls throughout the year. Given any date from the calendar, I should be able to predict with reasonable accuracy what I would find there. Yet, given the nature of time—the way it expands to encompass space and possibility—there will always be surprises. Over the years my garden has attracted toads, great-horned owls, Harris' hawks, roadrunners— all manner of animals that ordinarily shun the city. Given enough time, it might surprise me with a coyote, a desert tortoise, or even a great blue heron. The miracle of the garden is the miracle of diversity: given life, more life comes.

The uses of diversity, like those of adversity, are sweet. Any biologist can rattle off two or three without thinking. For example, a diverse community of plants and animals is in all likelihood a healthy community, one with a full array of trophic levels: carnivores, insectivores, herbivores, saprovores, omnivores, detritivores, and plants, all connected by a dense and complex web of interactions and dependencies. Remove a keystone species, and the entire community collapses. Take out the coyotes and mountain lions, and deer multiply to the point of starvation—and to the point of denuding the trees and shrubs they browse upon. Take out the bats, and mosquito populations boom. Take out mosquitoes, and the fish and frogs die off.

From our selfish human point of view, a diverse community is not only healthy, it is health-giving. Life-saving medicines like aspirin and digitalin were extracted from plants long before they were synthesized in laboratories. It has been suggested that the incalculable diversity of the Amazon rain forest holds many more such medicines as yet unknown—but only, of course, if the forest is allowed to thrive in its diverse entirety. Diverse communities provide health in other essential ways. A species-rich salt marsh, for instance—one with many kinds of rushes, sedges, grasses, waterfowl, fish, and mollusks—is capable of absorbing huge quantities of nutrients from sewage waste. What is filth to us is food for them, and salt marshes have become de facto sewage treatment facilities for the world's coastal cities. Thoreau wrote that in wilderness lies the preservation of the world. I would add a corollary: in diversity lies the preservation of the world.

Something in me—probably in all of us—craves diversity. It could be another vitamin or an essential micronutrient like zinc. When I hike above the tree line in the Sierra Nevada, a hundred nameless peaks—jagged blocks of stone and snow—loom above me. A mountain wind blows across my ears, deafening me to all sounds but that of my heart pounding in my veins. A raven's shadow undulates over the snow, then skims across a cliff, rushing up to meet the bird, and when he drops over the peak and out of sight, I am the only living creature in a landscape of terrible beauty and frightening inhumanity. The only thing I know at such moments is how out of place I am. Later, coming back down the trail to the land of the living, a place where jays squawk from lodgepole pines and bumblebees roister in the delphiniums, I return to nature on a human scale. Returning to a diversity of living forms, I return to myself, too.

Some people fulfill their daily diversity requirement by moving from spot to spot, tormented like Herman Melville with an everlasting itch for things remote. Like him, they love to sail forbidden seas and land on barbarous coasts. Others stay in one place, content to let time bring them the diversity they need. Thoreau comes to mind, of course: "The man who is often thinking that it is better to be somewhere else than where he is excommunicates himself," he said. He claimed he would rather watch cows in a pasture for a day than wander to Europe or Asia. "It is only ourselves that we report in either case," he explained, "and perchance we shall report a more restless and worthless self in the latter case than in the first."

Like Thoreau, I sometimes wonder what I will do once I learn all the plants and animals in my region. I could broaden my knowledge by traveling to new places and learning new names. This, I suppose, is partly the appeal of natural history expeditions to exotic places like the Galapagos Islands and the Antarctic. But traveling for new sights and experiences has this disadvantage: as a tourist you must always be moving on, so you never fully enter the life of the place, you never fully understand it, you never completely partake of all its nourishment. The other possibility is to stay where I am and deepen my knowledge. As a resident I have the luxury of time. I can soak down into the daily lives of plants and animals as unhurriedly as water soaks into loam.

Some say that Thoreau was a mama's boy, reluctant to remove himself too far from the nest. His love for Concord and environs, they say, merely made a virtue of necessity. But turning necessity into virtue is not necessarily a bad thing. Once in a while, when I find myself thinking that any other place would be better than this, when I feel intolerably constricted and hemmed in by my life, it's enough to step out into the garden. Instantly, I am in touch with larger spheres. My citrus trees and melons originated in the Middle East, my gerbera daisies in South Africa. My tomatoes came from South America by way of Mexico, a beneficent legacy of Cortez's otherwise brutal conquest. The Gila woodpecker squawking among the palm fronds reminds me of the encircling desert. The rufous hummingbird darting at the feeder connects me to points as distant as Alaska and Vera Cruz. My garden becomes the world at my doorstep.

That's when I realize that the natural paradise I seek is not in Hawaii or in the Sierra Nevada or anywhere else: it is right here in my own backyard where a verdin twitches on the telephone wire, ants make wobbly exclamation points as they march under pyracantha leaves held aloft, the dog next door rattles his dish, and wind chimes talk from yard to yard. This world may be objectively small, but I could spend a lifetime learning all about it. Its limits are as broad and deep as my understanding.

I pick up my journal again. A white-winged dove calls from the telephone wire, its voice throaty and muffled. He sounds as though his head is buried beneath a pillow. The watermelon vines silently plot to take over the backyard. Tiny blue butterflies spark from the zucchini plants. The scutter of an invisible bug under fallen leaves brings the cat to attention. If these ordinary miracles aren't enough, that's too bad, because this garden—this here and now—is all I've got. It's more than enough for a full life in a small place.

THE MOCKINGBIRD'S SONG

In the spring the mockingbird is his song, it seems. He warbles ceaselessly from every high point in the garden, spilling volumes of notes into the air as if wrapping his territory in sound. From time to time he flings himself upward, still singing. As he floats back down, wings spread, he tips from side to side like a falling leaf. On moonlit nights, his insomniac caroling rings in the stillness. Even in the day, he sings loud enough to cover every sound but the roar of jets overhead.

Sometimes—at the beginning of every breeding cycle— the male in my garden seems too busy singing to eat, as if performance itself were food enough. Half-hidden in foliage, he whisper-sings low, soft, sweet tones, inaudible except at close range. When I draw near, I can see his throat flutter. Within a week he will be singing at full volume. The paired phrases will follow one another without pause: the cactus wren's furious scolding will tumble upon the verdin's sweet-sweet, which in turn will merge with the curve-billed thrasher's whit-wheat. He will even imitate the distress cries of baby mockingbirds: "scree, scree, scree," he'll shriek, as though hurting or hungry.

Not every mockingbird song is a direct imitation. Many are brief improvisations, notes strung together more or less at random and never, or rarely, repeated that way again. It's said that a versatile male may have a repertoire of several hundred songs. I can never identify with certainty more than a few of the songs my mockingbird sings, but because every tune, whether imitation or original speech, is uttered in the same clear, clarion voice, unmistakably the tones of a mockingbird, even I can tell the difference between the imitations and the real thing.

Mockingbirds sing for the same reasons other birds sing: to acquire and defend territory and to stimulate the female at critical phases of her reproductive cycle. But, whereas most birdsong is rigidly patterned, the mockingbird repertoire is as individual as the words you or I might choose for a poem. No one really knows why, although complicated theories abound. All we know for certain is that female mockingbirds consistently choose mates who have the richest vocabularies, and male mockingbirds with the largest repertoires gain and keep the best territories.

Strangely, many ornithologists were long reluctant to allow the mockingbird his skills. It evidently went against the grain to allow a mere bird, supposedly a slave to instinct, even a modest degree of free will. "Inherited mimesis," one claimed, meaning that mockingbird song was inherent and hereditary. He thought that any resemblance to the song of actual birds was entirely in the listener's mind. His colleagues agreed. "Fortuitous similarity," they called it and suggested that the human ear insists on hearing resemblances where none exist, just as our brains assign plots to the random images in our dreams. The few ornithologists who were willing to admit that mockingbirds did indeed imitate actual birdsong quickly pointed out that mimicry was apparently "an aimless and useless art."

This skepticism could have been easily demolished by the simple expedient of raising a baby mockingbird by hand, which is what one Tennessee ornithologist finally did. She recorded its various utterances at regular intervals, from the first whisper song at four weeks to imitations of starlings, blue jays, flickers, cardinals, and several other species at five months. By its second year indoors, it had managed to pick up forty-two different songs of twenty-four different species, all neighborhood birds, as well as the mailman's whistle and the washing machine's squeak. Clearly, she concluded, mockingbirds build their repertoires gradually by imitating the birds they hear.

These are not stupid birds, after all. Alert and inquisitive, they keep tabs on everything in my garden, as watchful as a child in unfamiliar surroundings. They know one another, they know their offspring, they know the other birds who occupy my garden. They know their enemies, too. I read about an ornithologist who, in the course of a study on mockingbirds, had to handle eggs and nestlings, much to the distress of the parents. At first they hovered overhead and called in alarm, then, when that failed, they rushed at him whenever he came near the nest. He was the only person they attacked; casual passersby were left alone.

In just this way, the male mockingbird in my garden knows the cats of the neighborhood. Some he ignores, others—particularly Katie, my small, talkative tortoiseshell—he harasses mercilessly. Chiding in a rough voice, he dives at her again and again, narrowly missing her spine. Usually, she puts her ears back and slinks away. One time, though, I saw her leap right at him. She cleared the ground by a good two feet, but the mockingbird escaped. Greatly sobered, I would guess, he retreated to his perch and considered the matter in silence before he flew away.

I've never had the heart to keep statistics, but I'm sure that Katie tops the cats of Felversham, an English village where, over the course of a year, seventy-eight cats caught nearly eleven hundred birds, rodents, and other animals—a mere fourteen per cat. Katie catches several birds a week, a dozen in a month, easily a hundred each year. She is the suburban equivalent of a red fox or a great horned owl, top carnivores whose livelihoods depend on hunting skills.

Except that hers doesn't, of course, and at times I wonder at my attachment to her. As she trifles with her prey, her double nature troubles me. She seems cruel then, almost evil. Later, she gentles herself into my good graces—purrs when I approach, licks my arm, stretches herself across my lap, and sinks into sleep, a picture of love and malice. I wonder, too, at my sudden, tardy attachment to the house finches, ground doves, and English sparrows she brings to the doorstep in steady succession. When each was alive, it was only one of many in a group of indistinguishable small birds. But once Katie singles one out, it becomes an individual to me, and I feel sad even though I know that the living exist but to give up their lives to enable the living of others.

So food webs imply, anyway. A friend of mine eats no meat because she believes that life is sacred. I respect her views, but as a biologist I can't agree with them. Nature is profligate with life. Far from being sacred, it is the most expendable of commodities, as disposable as feathers or fingernails. Creatures procreate and are born in their millions, and of these only a tiny percentage survive to beget another generation. It is not life that is sacred, but the connections among living beings.

From the kitchen window, I watch as the male mockingbird sips from a dripping water faucet. By standing on tiptoe and stretching his neck, he can remove each drop as it beads up inside the spigot. Then I see that Katie, hunkered down under the overturned wheelbarrow, is watching, too. Her tail swishes, her haunches twitch. I rush outdoors, and the mockingbird flies away. "Bad kitty," I say, but it does no good. Something ancient and undeniable demands that she hunt, and no amount of scolding can quench the wild flame that trembles inside her.

This is especially true in the spring, when the mocking-bird fledglings, learning to fly and forage for themselves, are most vulnerable. This spring there are two. Their tails are stubby, their necks streaked with gray, their mouths lined with yellow. Plump and wedge-shaped, a marked contrast to their elegant, streamlined parents, they look unbalanced, and I constantly expect them to plop onto their faces. They beg incessantly, noisily, pitifully. Hunger envelops them. Their world consists of the pain in their guts and the reassuring flap of a parent's wings. As always, I think of how wearing it would be to be a bird parent. Not a moment's peace, always on call. One parent finds something—an earwig, most likely—and thrusts its bill into the young one's noisy mouth. The fledgling continues to beg, swallows, realizes it has been fed and is silent for a blessed second or two before it starts begging again. Its sibling pecks at likely looking objects in the dirt. Judging from the number of times it rejects its selections, it is not very successful. Sometimes the parents bring pyracantha berries, now ripe and plentiful, to their young. That's not right, I want to tell them; the young of most bird species are carnivores, not vegetarians. After a while, the begging stops. The fledglings sit among the dense branches of the pyracantha, and their parents perch on the phone line overhead. A quiet moment at last.

By good luck, I am on hand for many moments of their lives. The two adults often show up when I turn the compost pile and the ground is alive with insects as cockroaches, crickets, and earwigs flee in every direction. Perched nearby in the grapefruit tree, the mockingbirds eye the menu carefully and with nice discrimination pick out the earwigs. Sometimes they subdue their prey by prodding it against the dirt. The male is bolder than his mate. Often he forages on the pile itself and sometimes alights so close I could touch him with outstretched arm: he watches bugs with one eye and me with the other, ready to take flight. His mate, meanwhile, usually hangs back in the shadowy safety of the grapefruit tree until I turn away. In winter, two mockingbirds occasionally dance underneath the grape arbor. They face one another a foot or two apart and step to one side or the other, maintaining always the same distance. Mirroring one another's movements, they zigzag back and forth for five or ten minutes; then one flies off. In early spring, rival males battle in the air. They clash breast to breast with fanned wings, swoop after one another from tree to tree. A ritualized conflict yet real nonetheless. It's startling to realize the pitch at which they lead their lives over an ordinary suburban garden.

Bit by bit, and with the help of books, I begin to piece these unconnected incidents into a coherent picture. I read that the mockingbird pair in my garden will probably stay mated as long as both live. I find out that a combination of insects and fruits does no harm once the young birds are capable of maintaining their body temperatures without maternal brooding. It may even be more beneficial than a diet of insects alone, since fruits supply vitamins and minerals not found in insects. The breast-to-breast clashes are territorial disputes of the fiercest kind, it turns out, and the peculiar ballet under the grape arbor is a stylized version of the same thing. My morning walks, I realize, are strolls from one singing mockingbird to another. Their territories fit together like the pieces of a broken cup, a three-dimensional puzzle extending over the entire neighborhood. Although each pair holds its territory more or less permanently, the actual boundaries shift from season to season, probably to accommodate variations in food supply and nesting cover, thus the need for territorial battles.

Moving through their territory day to day, fortuitously present for many moments of their lives, I begin to feel that in some clumsy, half-instinctive way I know the mockingbird pair in my garden. We share salient characteristics, after all— warm blood, free will, oral communication, monogamy, parental care of young—but what really makes the difference is that they have become individuals to me. "My pair," is how I think of them. They recognize me, too. In fact, they knew me before I knew them, and every time I go outside, they follow me at a circumspect distance, gliding from the mulberry to the clothesline, from the clothesline to the fence, apparently convinced that any activity of mine is bound to result in food. By midsummer, my pair has produced a second set of young, which shriek all day long. Katie seems to understand that the fledglings are easier prey than the parents, and she watches them constantly. The male, as vigilant as the cat herself, swoops at her whenever she appears. She can hardly cross the street or venture down the alley without his scolding attendance, and she takes on a harried, hunted look.

Inevitably, she finds her opportunity at last and meows loudly to bring me to the back door. What I expect to see on the mat is a dead fledgling. What I see instead is the limp body of the male himself. He is surprisingly small and slender, as though death has reduced him by a third. Except for his head, flung aside at an impossible angle, he is perfect in every detail, from the feet like curved gray sickles to the white-edged tail feathers.

I weep, and, for the next few days, I avoid the garden. The sight of the mockingbird family, now reduced to three, makes my chest ache. I tell myself that this is nature's scheme. Birds catch earwigs, and cats—even well-fed ones—catch birds. But this fails to soothe. What matters now is not the balance of nature, but that particular bird, which had become an individual and therefore something precious to me.

If a pair of mockingbirds lays two eggs per clutch, two clutches per year, perhaps six or eight clutches over a lifetime, it is because out of these dozen or so eggs, only two will survive long enough to reproduce. Some will fall victim to the great-tailed grackle's lust for eggs. Others will hatch, but the nestlings will tumble from the nest or be killed by cats or hit by cars or die of disease. A few may survive all this yet lose out in the competition for mates. Despite this carnage, the mockingbird population remains in equilibrium: the number of eggs laid accommodates the degree of predation; the number of deaths is sufficient to prevent a population explosion. We might well conclude that it doesn't matter which individuals live or die—it only matters that some do.

Yes, but. Yes, but I cared about that individual mockingbird because I am an individual, too. Unlike the mockingbird and most other animals, we humans seem unable to maintain a reasonable balance between births and deaths. Yet, despite our gross numbers, a patent burden to the planet and to other life-forms, we insist on the supreme value of individual human lives, or say we do. Why else install artificial hearts in human chests, connect dying bodies to artificial lungs, freeze fertilized eggs for implantation into barren wombs, protest at the abortion of human embryos? We will balk at no expense to save or foster a human life, it seems, as long as we perceive that life as an individual person. The opposite—erasing the individual among faceless millions—enables us to calmly contemplate the deaths of young men and women in war, of families in earthquakes, of entire tribes in genocidal slaughter. By this same trick of the mind, we scarcely noticed the imminent extinction of the gray whale as a species, yet when three gray whales were trapped in arctic ice, we contributed thousands of dollars to their rescue and watched anxiously on television until their safety seemed assured. We loved the whales when they became individuals.

We love the individual because each of us is the star of her own drama, the center of her own universe. This, too, is good biology. Without individuals, evolution would never take place. If DNA were capable of replicating itself indefinitely without error, we would not exist. Life would consist of the same single-celled creatures that arose in the primordial sea. It is the capacity of DNA to err—to create an aberrant individual—that is the basis of natural selection and therefore evolution. Without variation, natural selection would have nothing to work upon, and all mockingbirds would sing identical songs. Without variation, there would be no individuals.

We must hold in our minds these utterly contradictory thoughts: not one of us matters at all; each of us is infinitely precious. This is the mockingbird's song.

TRANSFORMATIONS

When freshly hatched, a gulf fritillary caterpillar is a squiggle no more than a millimeter long and gives no hint of the elegant orange and silver-spangled butterfly it is destined to become. Tiny as it is, an even tinier object—a golden egg no larger than a pinhead—once contained it. Their minuscule volumes reflect a trade-off between size and safety. The caterpillar requires space as it develops inside the delicate shell, yet the egg becomes more and more visible to predators as its dimensions increase. The compromise results in a caterpillar so small that when I bring it indoors on a passionflower leaf I need not cover the jar, not yet, for its world is thoroughly circumscribed by the leaf itself.

I did this as a child, too—searched for caterpillars on weeds and caged them in jars—but they never thrived under my lackadaisical care. Now that my attention span is longer, I remember to keep my charge well supplied with fresh leaves, which it devours in ever-increasing amounts. By its tenth day of life, my gulf fritillary caterpillar—at first smooth and grublike—has developed a spiky coat. It becomes a regular Christopher Columbus, and over the course of a day it

promenades the full length and breadth of its leaf, taking delicate nibbles from the margin and leaving pinpoint dots of
black frass.

A caterpillar has no sexual organs and little in the way of
senses. It sees light, responds to gravity and clasps surfaces, all
in the service of its major activity—eating. This is its raison
d'être, really. With its large jaws and huge gut, a caterpillar *is*
a feeding stage, a way of ingesting enough plant material to
create the reproductive adult. How much will it eat? Quite a
bit in the case of a tobacco hornworm, which devours nearly
three square feet of tobacco leaves during its larval existence,
less in the case of smaller caterpillars, which have less biomass
to produce.

The more a caterpillar eats, the faster it grows, and every
few days it outgrows its skin, which must then be shed. For
the gulf fritillary this is an easy, matter-of-fact process: the
caterpillar clings to the underside of a leaf and literally crawls
out of its skin bit by bit. All that's left is a fringe of black
spines. For the pipevine swallowtail, however, the shedding
of skin is time-consuming and immobilizing. As contractions ripple from its tail to its head, the caterpillar thrashes its
forequarters from side to side for several minutes, then, seem-
ingly half-crippled, begins to inch forward like a mermaid
on dry land. I imagine it's like trying to remove a turtleneck
sweater without using your hands. As it crawls, the bright,
glossy colors of the tight new skin appear near the head, and
the loose old skin migrates toward the tail where it accumu-
lates in folds like a nylon stocking gathered between a pair
of hands. Until the caterpillar frees itself from these fetters,
it is highly vulnerable, trapped between the old stage and the
new, easy pickings for a bird or wasp.

Five times in fifteen days my gulf fritillary caterpillar
changes its skin. Five times it is swept up in sensations it
cannot influence, understand, or anticipate, like a Victorian

woman in labor for the first time. The sixth time is different as the chemical soup in its brain stops producing juvenile hormone. This signals the end of the eating phase. The next stage will not be a larger, still more voracious caterpillar, but a resting phase—a chrysalis.

At first I'm afraid that my caterpillar is sick. It attaches its hindmost feet to a twig with silk, then hangs head down in a J shape. For twelve hours it remains absolutely immobile. Worried because captive caterpillars are susceptible to fungal and viral attack, I fidget with the furnishings of its cage: change the damp rag, add fresh leaves, scrub out every vestige of mold or mildew. The caterpillar does not respond, and when I notice that its lavender and maroon stripes are fading to grayish white, I realize why. Pupation has begun.

As the stripes continue to fade, the caterpillar discolors, like a vegetable being visibly overgrown by mold. By degrees, more slowly than water creeps up a paper towel, a white veil envelops the head. It reminds me of the cowls donned by death-row inmates right before execution. The caterpillar shudders as contractions pass from head to toe. The purpose of the contractions, it soon appears, is to gather the old skin around the tail end. This done, the skin itself must be jettisoned, and for a full minute the caterpillar twists and writhes like a hula dancer. Over the next hour, the white veil spreads to the tail, forming a pronounced dorsal hump. I can see nothing of the caterpillar now: its feet have disappeared, its tail is indistinguishable from its head. In fact, the caterpillar as such no longer exists. It trembles slightly and continuously, like a vase shaken by vibrations from a passing train. Within a few hours more, the trembling has stopped and the transformation from cylindrical caterpillar to spindle-shaped chrysalis is complete.

Riveted, aghast, dumbfounded, I can hardly believe or comprehend what I have seen. What began as a game, a playful extension of childhood experiments, becomes unexpectedly serious, something more than a way of making a full life in a small place. There is something here that I must understand.

I remember Greek myths learned in high school. Dryope, gathering lotus flowers, is startled when the freshly cut stems drip blood. The plant is in reality a transformed nymph. Despite Dryope's ignorance, the gods transform her into a tree as punishment. She becomes rooted to the ground and cannot move; in anguish she tears her hair and finds her hands full of leaves. Her infant feels its mother's breast harden, and the milk ceases to flow. Dryope's last act is to kiss her baby goodbye before bark entombs her face.

Obsessed with transformation, which they saw all around them but could not explicate, the ancient Greeks turned to mythology, a haphazard amalgam of hopeful explanations, historical recollections, and cautionary tales. Fleeing Apollo, who has more than a kiss in mind, Daphne cries to the river god for help. Immediately her limbs become stiff, bark encloses her breasts, her hair turns leafy, and she, too, is a tree. Jealous Hera changes Callisto into a bear, and then Zeus makes her a constellation. Actaeon, unlucky enough to witness Diana bathing, is turned into a deer, whereupon his own hunting dogs tear him to pieces.

These transformations never, it seems, lead to something else—they are not a resting stage, like the chrysalis, but an end. Were such stories a way to think about the ultimate transformation from life to death? The ancient Greek word for butterfly, *psyche*, was also their word for soul. The soul was immortal, they believed, and so, in a way, was the butterfly's resurrection from a deathlike pupal stage. But we have no immortal soul, only a beleaguered psyche, and, as far as I can tell, this single life is the only one we're given. Perhaps this is why I am intent on transformation: to turn one life into many, to postpone as long as possible its inevitable ending.

Hoping for further understanding, I bring a series of caterpillars indoors, half a dozen or more over the course of the
summer. I cage them, feed them, make notes and comparisons. Gulf fritillary caterpillars, it appears, do little overt to
prepare for pupation; they simply hang in place and wait for
the inevitable. Caterpillars of pipevine swallowtails, on the
other hand, undertake vast (for a caterpillar) migrations in
search of a proper place to pupate. Some wander for as long
as eighteen hours before they settle. Mine alternates bursts
of speed with sluglike torpor in its peregrination of the jar.
The giant swallowtail caterpillar puts on a trapeze act: after
attaching its hindmost feet to a twig with silk, it spins a guyline from the twig to the center of its body; once securely
anchored, it flings its head back like a flamenco dancer and
pupates in the shape of the letter L. The white-lined sphinx
moth, like all of its kind, pupates underground as a cocoon.
My sphinx moth caterpillar, using only its head and upper
body, tediously excavates a walnut-sized burrow in the damp
earth I have provided. Terrible to be caught without a burrow,
to feel oneself changing before all is in readiness.

These chrysali are the first I've ever seen. As I child, I
searched on stems, stalks, weathered boards, and brush piles
but never found one. (I lacked the ingenuity of two clever
entomologists who raised pipevine caterpillars in the laboratory, then, after the fifth molt, marked them with fluorescent paint, followed them through the woods to their chosen
pupation sites, then collected the chrysali the following night
with the aid of an ultraviolet lamp.) Each chrysalis formed
under my care mimics some natural object, some bit of nature
too small, too withered, too distasteful to bother about. The
giant swallowtail chrysalis is only somewhat more attractive than the caterpillar itself, which closely resembles a bird
dropping. Colored a dullish brown, flecked with roughened
patches, the chrysalis can hardly be distinguished from a

bit of wood. The disguise is imperfect at first: when newly formed, the pupa inside responds to light and jarring movements. Like a houseplant, it will point toward the nearest window, and like a cat, it startles when bumped. Once the resting phase is fully engaged, though, it remains inert, apparently as lifeless as the twig it mimics. Light gray with sooty streaks, the gulf fritillary chrysalis could be a curled leaf on a dead twig, ready to drop at any moment. The chrysalis of the giant clouded sulphur is sunflower yellow when fresh, then fades to pale green, a folded leaf instead of a flower. Pipevine swallowtail chrysali may be green or brown, depending on whether the caterpillar has selected a smooth surface, like a stem, on which to pupate, or a rough one, like a stick or a rock. A credible disguise is crucial; if the caterpillar is vulnerable during molting and pupation, it is even more vulnerable as a chrysalis, when it can neither escape nor defend itself. Invisibility is its first and final line of defense.

Sometimes referred to as a "resting phase," the chrysalis is actually a metamorphic bridge between caterpillar and butterfly, and while its exterior remains perfectly static, the pupa inside is furiously changing. From the beginning, every caterpillar possesses a group of cells called imaginal discs. Once pupation is complete, these cells begin to divide, forming rudimentary adult features—wing stubs, mouthparts, thoracic muscles, legs. Development proceeds at a rapid pace: my gulf fritillary spends merely eight days as a chrysalis, my pipevine swallowtail just twelve. The only exterior sign of these internal changes comes at the end, when the chrysalis darkens perceptibly, not because the husk itself has changed color but because the butterfly inside, now fully formed and ready to emerge, shows through the thin shell like a hand seen through fine china. An anatomist could track the transformation by making cross-sections of chrysali of different ages. Under a microscope, she could see the organs and tissues develop as larvaldom receded. Often I wish that I could peek under the skin to see the whole organism as it changes, the way sound waves can show a fetus developing in its mother's uterus. But I can't. All I can do is try to imagine the surpassing oddity of being one kind of creature on the outside and an entirely different one on the inside.

Although butterfly collectors sometimes raise caterpillars so that they can kill and mount the freshly emerged butterfly before it fades and tears, I am not an accumulator of dead insects. My great fear is of coming home from work to find a dying butterfly imprisoned in the jar where I had left a chrysalis. I remember what Colette wrote about her mother: "In her life there was never the memory of a dishonored wing, and if she trembled with longing in the presence of a closed calyx, a chrysalis still rolled in its vanished cocoon, at least she respectfully awaited the moment. How pure are those who have never forced anything open!" As a child, Colette discovered to her anguish that the creature pried too early from its pupa is neither one thing nor the other, neither caterpillar nor butterfly, and is not suited for either life. Once opened, it can neither advance to the next stage nor return to its former state. It has no equipment for repairing its damaged covering nor yet has it wings for flying. "I thwarted the blind purpose of the bilious-looking, black-brown chrysalis," she wrote, "and hurled it from its temporary death into a final nothingness."

So, even though my fingers itch every time I pass the jar where the sphinx moth pupated, I leave it strictly alone. There's no sign of activity, not even a ruffling of the soil above the burrow. Every so often I glance at the jar, almost fearful of what I'll see, afraid that whatever is there will be so horrible I'll have to avert my eyes. A Caliban, perhaps, a transformation gone awry. This is, I realize then, one of our primal fears: if we examine ourselves too closely, we'll find unspeakable Calibans; examine ourselves too soon, we'll be frozen in place like pupae aroused before their time.

As soon as each chrysalis forms, I place it outdoors in a safe place. Instead of returning to captive butterflies, I come home time after time to empty chrysali, tattered shells as insubstantial as ancient paper. Evidently, I am fated never to see the husk actually split, never to watch the crimped and sodden butterfly creep from its shelter. But at least I am on hand to watch a recently emerged pipevine swallowtail discover its new form. The butterfly hangs motionless from its twig, uncoils its tongue, pumps its wings weakly. The wings are always crumpled upon emergence, and it takes some time for them to harden as lymph flows into the veins. Even so, I can hardly believe that this wide-winged insect could have fit inside such a tiny case. It is all I can do to keep myself from touching the tender wings to see how they feel. The swallowtail's large black eyes show no reflective surface—blind eyes, I would think, except that when I bend too close, it flinches. For long minutes, it does not move, and I wonder if it is somehow damaged. Perhaps if I shift its twig from shadow into sunlight. . . As I do so, the startled butterfly spreads its wings and rises straight to the upper branches of the mulberry tree overhead. I feel appropriately reproved. Swallowtails have been emerging for millions of years, it seems to tell me, and we don't require any help from you.

Other than this small insight, I have little to show for my careful observations. After recording the metamorphosis of half a dozen butterflies and moths, I am no wiser than the insect physiologist who whirs pupae of various ages in her blender and analyzes the extract for its chemical constituents. Transformation, it would seem, does not lie solely in the relative proportions of this hormone to that, nor is it merely a matter of minutes spent writhing, hanging, resting, pumping. It is both simpler and more profound. Transformation is the evolutionary solution to limitations imposed by insect morphology.

Sluggish, sedentary, purblind, the larva is ill-equipped for defending itself and finding mates but admirably adapted for sitting in one spot and feeding and growing. The adult lepidopteran is a limited feeder: its slender proboscis, a capillary tube, permits ingestion of liquids only. This liquid diet, sufficient to keep a butterfly going for its allotted week or two of life, would be too meager to sustain the lengthy development from caterpillar to pupa to adult. On the other hand, its wings give the butterfly great mobility, an advantage in seeking out mates and eluding birds, lizards, and other hazards. But how did the larva get to be a butterfly? Many millions of years ago, the larval form of an insect was little different from the adult. (We see this still in certain insects like grasshoppers and cicadas.) Complete metamorphosis, involving the four discrete stages of egg, larva, pupa, and adult, evolved about 330 million years ago (some 70 million years before the first butterflies appeared). It is thought that aquatic larvae, which had gills for breathing underwater, sometimes used their gills to glide through the air, an expedient way to escape predators or to search for food. Over the eons, gills turned into flaps, and flaps turned into wings. One good thing generally leads to another in evolution, and this time it led to a gulf between the larval and the adult stages. Division of labor provided the perfect solution to morphological limitations: larvae could specialize in eating, adults in mating, and the pupa—the chrysalis—could provide the bridge between the two.

This is the perpetual wonder of transformation: the individual remains the same since its genetic make-up does not change, yet the gulf between caterpillar and butterfly is complete. The voraciously feeding caterpillar has no intimations of the free-flying transformation to come; the butterfly has no *nostalgie de la boue* for those sedentary days of mindless gluttony.

Apparently, we believe in transformation as deeply as we believe in anything, so we forget we are not like the moth or the butterfly. The slow, steady turnover of our body cells is not even visible, yet somehow fat baby legs turn slender and deerlike, rosebud nipples become full-blown breasts, white hairs replace brown, freckled skin covers smooth. This is metamorphosis, too, but we fail to see the miracle in it, which is the same as for the butterfly: no matter how varied the incarnation, the inhabitant remains the same. No matter how many times or how much we change, we bring our selves—our histories—with us.

So appealing is transformation—this vision of new form and new life—that we build it into our dearest beliefs. Reincarnation myths suggest that again and again we are reborn to new lives, new selves, new problems, each bringing us one step closer to eventual release from the chain of transformation. The life of Christ embodied the transformation to end all transformations: he took on human form, then became divine again, a prototype for the ultimate transformation of the true believer, who, like the sphinx-moth caterpillar, must not be caught unprepared.

In Greek mythology, transformation occurs most often as punishment or escape, and it's hard to say whether the change is an improvement or not. Callisto, turned by Hera into a bear, then by Zeus into a constellation, exchanges the passion and enterprises of earthly life for celestial immobility; Daphne eludes rape only by submitting to a kind of death in life. As appealing as transformation is in the abstract, we are profoundly ambivalent about its reality. Like Saint Augustine, who prayed, "Give me chastity and continence but not just now," we beg, "Let me change wholly but don't make me different."

We hunger for transformation as, after a week in the wilderness, we hunger for fresh fruit or leafy vegetables. At the beginning of every year, we take the first steps: we resolve to quit smoking, prevaricating, drinking, fornicating, to start jogging, meditating, dieting. We will, through our own dogged efforts, become better persons, or at least different. As individuals, we seem intent on a vision quest, yet our culture has failed to institutionalize the search. Left to our own devices, we haunt psychologists in the hope of transformation: perhaps they can teach us how to break with a destructive past, to express love or anger, to forgive our enemies and ourselves. We enroll in twelve-step programs; we take seminars in Zen. Our culture has become remarkable for the contrast between the degree of enlightenment supposedly possible and that actually realized.

Latter-day saints, we seek transformation in wild, lonely places, taking as our model one Henry David Thoreau. The little cabin built from scrap lumber, the clearing planted to pole beans, Walden Pond visible as blue stripes between vertical tree trunks, and Thoreau himself in the midst of it all, communing with fish, birds, turtles, clouds, minerals, rivers and hailstones—it all sticks in our minds like cockleburs to wool socks. We weakly imitate him every time we don backpacks or load canoes for a week in the wilderness. If Walden Pond was Thoreau's vision quest, this is ours, as close as most of us get to the Plains Indians' search for the one dream, the one illumination, that suffices for the remainder of our lives.

I come home from a day-long outing, glance as usual inside the jar where the cocoon lies hidden. A sphinx moth, a brown-and-white-mottled triangle, lies perfectly still on the surface of the soil. The individual wing scales are like short, thick, soft hairs, but the moth does not move. The pinkish patches on the hindwings are nearly covered by the overlapping forewings, but the moth does not seem alive. I grab the jar, rush outside, tear off the cheesecloth cover. Extending a finger into the jar, I touch the moth gently and nearly cry as it shudders, then shoots out of the jar, across the yard, and out of sight.

My relief is a measure of the fear I had harbored—my fear that the soil would produce not a living moth but an inert object. Only now do I understand that the fear of transformation is always present because the need for transformation is always present, too. I have in too many ways become the adult I never wanted to be: lacking in grace, intelligence, wit; guilty of many small crimes; at times barely worthy of respect and love. As much as I have changed already, my life still cries out for transformation.

Despite evidence to the contrary, I persistently believe that moving to a new place will change my life. It seems as logical as a legal argument, at times, as if I were requesting a change of venue for a fair trial. Unbiased jurors, is that what I'm looking for? Or maybe, exhausted from self-criticism, what I want is an unbiased judge, someone to tell me that if I am worse than I know, I am also better.

Whether rapid or slow, the process of transformation is mysterious, unyielding, much less susceptible to force of will than we might we wish. Examining the past helps. Accepting ourselves as we are, difficult as that may be, helps, too. So does solitude, sometimes. So, once in a great while, does retreat. We need to remember, however, that the transformations that last are apt to be the ones achieved in the midst of daily life. Woven into the fabric of who we are and where we live, they demand less in the way of sainthood, more in the way of simply living full lives in small spaces.

I stare across the yard. The last time I saw it, the sphinx moth was a green worm laboring to hollow out a little room underground. And now it takes off without a backward glance, intent only on the business of being an adult, its past life as completely forgotten as if it never happened. Not forgotten, really, but obliterated in the wholesale remakings of metamorphosis. For us there can be no gulf. We can transform ourselves only if we are willing to remember. Only in the presence of the past can we grow wings.

VULNERABILITIES

The leaf-cutter ants fly early in the morning, always the day after a summer rainstorm. I'm an early riser, too, but not early enough to catch the beginning of the mating flight when winged males and females swarm out of the nest, take to the air, mate, and disperse. By the time I enter my garden, what remains of the ant colony—thousands of ants, it seems—is milling about on the ground, an active red-brown blanket, and most of the winged forms are long gone. A few stragglers surge into the air, bumping into anyone or anything in their path; others, perhaps with defective wings, struggle in vain to leave the ground. I remember how one morning last summer, taking my daily run, I dashed through a dozen airborne ant swarms. Their fluttering wings in the sunlight looked like tiny bow ties. Soon after the mating flight, the males, their sole reason for existence now fulfilled, die. Each female, as she departs, has been impregnated for life. Her ovaries contain enough eggs to create a colony as large as the one she is leaving behind, and when she descends she will chew or rub her wings off, dig a small nest and begin to lay eggs fertilized with stored sperm.

The mating flight is a vulnerable time for the ants. Often they die of desiccation or starve. Many fall into puddles and drown. Others land on hard or rocky ground where they cannot excavate a nest. Occupied with mating and managing wings, they have little attention to spare for predators, and birds and frogs snap up many of them. In fact, I half expect to see a horned lizard taking advantage of this inside-out ant colony—ants are their primary food—but the one who haunts my garden is nowhere around. Perhaps the early morning hours are too chilly for a cold-blooded reptile.

Later in the day I *do* see him, and I crouch some distance away to watch. His mottled coloring—tan and beige and brown—makes him nearly invisible on the bare ground. Somewhat smaller than the palm of my hand, he has a pancake body, a short tail, and a rhomboidal head. He could be the invention of some medieval bestiarist. Conical spines ornament his back, and there's a dense fringe of spines where body meets ground. On his head, a row of backward-pointing spines like acacia thorns would stick in the throat of any predator incautious enough to swallow him. Only his belly is smooth, a vulnerable contrast to the formidable armature of head and back.

The horned lizard sits as still as a stone while a line of leaf-cutter ants files beneath his nose. A few of the ants palpate the underside of his jaw with tiny feelers. His eyes sink slowly closed. The heat of a summer afternoon soaks into both of us. Nearby, there is a characteristic horned lizard turd, a mahogany-colored cylinder about two inches long. I crumbled one once; it consisted, apparently, of shiny berry seeds that upon closer examination turned out to be ant parts so realistic I thought they might reassemble themselves and walk away. Maybe this horned lizard has already eaten his fill of ants. After five minutes he opens his eyes and watches the ant parade. Most of the ants are carrying bits of faded pink zinnia petals, which they've harvested from the compost pile. One ant, carrying nothing, isolated from the others, comes too close. In an instant, the pink tongue shoots out and the ant is gone. The lizard closes his eyes again, while the other ants, completely oblivious, continue to file past.

Ants fly in the morning, termites in the afternoon. There's a thunderstorm, and I'm standing at the screen door watching rain soak into the garden when I become aware of erratic raindrops flying counter to gravity. No, not rain, I decide in a moment, but a "hatch" of some sort. Grabbing an umbrella, I dash outside in time to see hundreds of termites boiling out of tiny holes in the ground. Termites are pale and fleshy, a kind of bleached-out ant. Some are winged; these clamber to the tiptops of grass blades and loft themselves into the air. Many are quickly battered back to the ground by raindrops as large as themselves, but some keep going, across the street, over the neighbor's house and out of sight. For every dozen that leave, another dozen, both winged and wingless, are squirming out of the holes.

This is a vulnerable time for them, too. Termites generally stay hidden underground where they are protected from predators. Their mating flight exposes them to these and other hazards. As I watch, small black ants appear and scurry about, grappling with the wingless termites and attempting to carry them off. Birds perch on wet roofs and in the watery street, picking up as many fallen termites as they can find. Winged forms still scrambling on the ground are snapped up with enormous relish by the horned lizard. Wheeling and scampering in pursuit of his prey, he moves with more alacrity than I've ever seen him display. I suppose that termites must be quite a delicacy for him since, unlike ants, they are soft-bodied and unable to bite or sting. Whenever he opens his wide triangle of a mouth, I can see its pink lining. He all but smacks his lips as he feeds—what a happy little guy.

Later, after the storm has passed, I go outside again. There's no sign of termites or of their below-ground colony; all the emergence holes have been sealed over, and I can't tell where they were. The horned lizard is gone, too.

With their spiny carapaces and devilish appearance, horned lizards are meant to convey an air of menace. It works surprisingly well—better with cats than with cars, though, and when I find the horned lizard near the street, I move him to safety. They're so slow that they're not hard to catch with bare hands, and their formidable spines are merely raspy against your palm and fingers. Soon afterwards, I notice Katie the cat staring intently at something in the garden. It is the horned lizard. She bats at it, and it raises itself on all four legs and darts right at her. Surprised, she backs off, and the lizard lowers itself to the ground. They sit about two feet apart and eye one another. Both would stay there all day, I suppose, except that I lure the cat inside with the promise of cheese. Later, I see her again contemplating the horned lizard with what appears to be curiosity tempered with respect; she's not accustomed to having her prey strike back. Good, I say to myself. He's safe from the cat, at least.

But not, it turns out, from me.

Walking by the empty compost bin, I see the horned lizard caught in the chicken wire. His head is all the way through one hole, and his front feet have clambered through the wire, too. The rest of his body sits outside the mesh, like Winnie the Pooh stuck in Rabbit's burrow. I stroke his back, expecting him to burst forward or backward, either aggravating his predicament or extricating himself entirely, but he does not move. He really *is* stuck. With infinite caution and delicacy,

I manipulate his legs until they are free. Releasing his head is trickier because the backward-pointing spines keep catching on the wire. By turning the body, I am able at last to slip his head out vertically, and then I see it, a dark wound, a gaping pocket in his belly. There's a stench. He is dead and beginning to putrefy.

How did it happen? Cat first, then a mad dash into the chicken wire? Or caught in the mesh, then ripped by the cat? Either way, the lizard might have been better off taking his chances with cars. Paradise is a dangerous place, and if I'm supposed to be God, I'm falling down on the job. It was a dubious kindness that prompted me to move him from the front to the back in the first place. My husband tries to console me. "You're too soft-hearted," he says, "and that's *not* a flaw." But I know better. I know that I acted out of pure self-ishness. I shepherded the horned lizard because I was afraid to find him squashed flat against the pavement. I was afraid to feel that pain. This is *my* vulnerability.

Over and over again I learn that to open my garden to life is also to open it to death. A thousand winged ants die before a single queen founds a new colony. The termites, for however brief a period, forsake the damp dark safety of their under-ground tunnels and come into the light where it is certain most will perish. New possibilities collide with old vulnera-bilities. To open ourselves to love is to open ourselves to pain, and to open ourselves to pain is to ensure the possibility of love.

THE EYE OF THE DRAGONFLY

"The thing about a fish pond," my friend Jeanne tells me, "is that you get all these hitchhikers you didn't even know you were bringing into your garden." She is right. Every pot of cattail and every flotilla of water hyacinth arrives with its own population of visible and invisible inhabitants: delicate triangles of water fern, dots of duckweed, snail eggs like gouts of transparent jelly, shrimplike larvae the color of filmy water, flatworms like slivers of animated mud.

Other water-lovers arrive under their own power, like the dragonflies and damselflies—big orange skimmers that zigzag over the garden or perch as motionless as hummingbirds; small blue dragonflies with transparent, gold-veined wings. Over the course of the summer, I spend hours watching them. Poised on the tip of a twig, wings spread wide, tail pointed slightly upwards, the blue dragonfly swivels its head from side to side with short, jerky movements like a mechanical toy. As a paper wasp cruises by, the dragonfly dashes out to investigate, then returns. A giant swallowtail wobbles overhead, and he darts after it, too.

In the afternoons, the orange skimmer performs figure eights above Katie the cat, each evidently considering the other as a potential meal. Dragonflies are fierce predators: one kind is even known as the mosquito hawk, which is not so much fierce as ludicrous—like using a bazooka to arrest a jaywalker. This one makes no attempt to capture Katie, though. I guess he's not a cat hawk. In fact, I never see him catch anything. Like the blue dragonfly, he seems more interested in darting at the butterflies and hummingbirds that pass his perch—territorial rather than hunting behavior. Or perhaps he regards every winged creature as a potential mate until it proves otherwise.

One hot summer afternoon six vermilion damselflies materialize at my pond. They are fragile-looking insects with toothpick bodies. Their wings are a lacy network of vermilion veins. A mated pair, male in front with the female cantilevered beneath him, hemstitch their way around the perimeter. They pause for the male to grasp any convenient leaf as the female lowers the tip of her abdomen into the water. I don't know which is more amazing—that these six winged insects found one another or that they located this tiny body of water amidst a desert of houses and city streets.

Somehow they managed, though, and did so without benefit of smell or hearing. Damselflies and dragonflies are creatures of sight. The worlds of odor and sound do not exist for them. A dragonfly is essentially a pair of eyes, a visual apparatus accompanied as if by afterthought with brain, digestive system, and reproductive organs. Since dragonflies can see movement at a distance of sixty feet or more, they are extraordinarily difficult to capture. Alert and wary, the dragonflies in my garden spring into the air as I approach, then zigzag overhead like cue balls caroming off the cushions. The best way to catch one, entomologists say, is to study its flight path and await your opportunity near its regular perching station. If you are perfectly still, the dragonfly might not notice you. I am delighted to find that this is indeed the case. When I stand motionless, the orange skimmer accepts me as part of the landscape, an innocuous shrub or tree. This is all well and good, yet I can't help wondering why such a keen-sighted insect should be unable to tell a person from a plant.

Long before I had dragonflies, I had an optical device marketed as a dragonfly's eye. It was essentially a small cone with an eyepiece at one end and a faceted viewing field at the other. Looking through it, you saw a cubistic world, every object fractured into twenty-four angled images, every image containing recognizable parts but disassociated from the whole in a most disturbing fashion. *I* found it disturbing, anyway, and wondered how dragonflies felt about it.

The human eye is a single facet; the dragonfly eye is thousands of facets (up to ten thousand in certain species), each abutted against the next to form a hemisphere, like the triangles that make up a geodesic dome. The advantage of the compound eye—which is characteristic of all insects, not just dragonflies—is a wide field of view. With their multi-faceted eyes, dragonflies have ample warning of the approach of predators and therefore much more opportunity to locate prey themselves. But the disadvantages, it seemed to me, must be tremendous: if your faceted vision presented you with a thousand mosquitoes at once, how would you know which one to catch?

The answer lies in the structure of the dragonfly's eye. The first scientists who studied insect vision assumed that each facet supplied a tiny portion of the overall picture, like a single tile in a mosaic: put them all together and you have vision. But, as it turns out, facets are not two-dimensional structures. A group of facets is more like a handful of pencils than a mosaic of tiles. Each facet is a light-gathering and light-focusing device that works independently of the rest. If a wasp passes by, an image of it is formed in each facet, but the purpose of the facets is less to form pictures than it is to concentrate light into a narrow beam. Taken together, all the facets in an eye produce a mosaic of light—spots of light of differing intensity, each spot coming from a different portion of the wasp.

Dragonflies have what insect physiologists call "fast" vision: their eyes respond quickly to changes in light intensity and can perceive several hundred flickers per second. Insects with slow vision—butterflies and grasshoppers, for instance—see only forty or fifty flickers per second. Beyond that point, it's all a blur. The real purpose of the compound eye is to perceive movement, and that's why the dragonflies in my garden were so quick to chase flying insects but so slow to detect my stationary presence.

Humans think of vision as an instantaneous process. When we open our eyes, we see space, not time. It's different for dragonflies. Compound eyes translate form in space into events in time. The faster the eye, the more acute the translation, which is why dragonflies and other insects that hunt on the wing are able to perceive a moving object well enough to capture it.

To us, a wasp is a solid object in space. To a dragonfly, the wasp is a series of flickers in time. I keep thinking about that difference; I keep wondering what it would be like to see time.

A gulf fritillary, an orange butterfly with silver-spangled wings, dances around the passionflower vine in my garden. She is so absorbed in her task she doesn't notice me as I creep close enough to touch her. She touches down on a leaf, then springs up immediately. Up and down the twining stems she flutters; finally she grasps a free-floating tendril and, as it sinks beneath her slight weight, she curls the tip of her abdomen and dabs it against the stalk, depositing a golden droplet. This egg and the others she lays will hatch into squiggly, black caterpillars capable of surviving only on passionflower leaves.

The caterpillar is little more than a stomach attached to a minimal brain. Yet even this most basic of organisms has a sense of taste. I once put caterpillars of the white-lined sphinx moth on tomato leaves to see what they would do. The merest touch assured them that this was not a proper food, and they prowled about the pan in search of something better to eat.

As much delight as it brings us, we humans rely less on our sense of taste than on any other, I suppose. Taste is not as crucial to survival as sight and touch and hearing. Our language reflects these priorities. A person without sight is blind; a person without hearing is deaf; but we have no common English word for a person who cannot taste. Such people exist, though: I read somewhere about a man, a cancer patient, who had all but lost his sense of taste. Mostly he ate steaks grilled black and fiercely salted—that was the only food he could still savor. This lack—this senselessness—would be fatal for some species. The gulf fritillary, landing on a passionflower leaf, scratches the surface with the most delicate of touches (if she landed on your hand, you wouldn't feel her presence), yet this prick is enough to release the leaf's chemical signature. That's how she knows whether the plant is an appropriate host for her offspring.

Here—in the cancer patient and the butterfly—we witness the opposite ends of the spectrum: hard to believe that it's even the same sense. I am much closer to the man who ate blackened steaks than I am to the nimble-footed butterfly. What would it be like, I wonder, to tread upon a flavor?

It's no exaggeration to say that butterflies evolved through their sense of taste. The diversity of butterflies (and of plant-eating insects, in general) rests squarely on their ability to distinguish among the thirty thousand natural chemicals present in the plant kingdom. It's equally accurate to say that there'd be no need for thirty thousand different chemical compounds if not for the extraordinary diversity of insects—some three million species, give or take a million or two. This iterative process of proposition and response has been called chemical warfare. It's an example of coevolution, the complicated process that has given us, among other wonders, bats that hunt moths by sonar and moths capable of jamming the signals bats emit.

Almost any plant you can name contains an arsenal of noxious substances whose sole purpose is to deter insect attack. Plants in the mustard family, for example—cabbage, broccoli, cauliflower, kale—fairly brim with glucosinolates, a class of natural pesticides. Since few insects can eat these highly toxic compounds, the broccoli and cabbage in my garden are generally pest-free with the exception of small, green caterpillars. These are the larvae of the cabbage white, a common cool-season butterfly. Camouflaged by color and habit, they nibble the large, lobed leaves of broccoli into something more like split-leaf philodendrons and tunnel neatly into the hearts of Chinese cabbage. Using special enzymes in the gut, cabbage whites detoxify glucosinolates as they feed, negating the mustard family's best chemical weapon.

Not its only weapon, though. Many mustards contain additional compounds—cardenolides, cucurbitacins, alkaloids

—that specialist feeders avoid. This chemical arsenal evidently evolved as a second line of defense once the glucosinolate barrier had been penetrated. And so it goes, like the intricate footwork of a deadly boxing match—left hook, right jab, punch, and counterpunch.

Or is it more like a dance, a graceful waltz, two partners swirling in tandem, each responding to the slightest pressure of a glance, a hand, an arm?

I see a flash of iridescent blue as sunlight glances off the black wings of a pipevine butterfly. To judge by the desperate way she skims over the ground, she is hunting for a place to lay her eggs. She cruises over the coreopsis, the verbena, the lantana, but doesn't land. None have the arrow-shaped leaves she is searching for. Flickering through a gap in the fence, she passes from the garden to the alley. This is where the pipevines grow, pressed to the ground in the gravel and weeds. She skims over a small pipevine, returns, circles the plant. Almost reluctantly, she touches down upon a leaf, springs up immediately, circles again. A mistake could be fatal to her offspring. Yet the need to lay eggs presses ever more strongly, a compulsion not to be denied. She alights on the pipevine one more time, and, wings beating, touches tip of abdomen to leaf.

No mistake this time. Errors do occur, though, usually with fatal results for the caterpillars. Two patient lepidopterists watched a pipevine swallowtail lay hundreds of eggs on dozens of pipevines. But, after two weeks of faultless effort, she became so habituated to the characteristic arrow-head leaves (or so exhausted from her own unrelenting fecundity) that vision overrode taste, and she oviposited on smilax, a vine with similar leaves. An understandable error but a fatal one for her offspring: pipevine larvae do not survive on smilax.

Not all oviposition errors are fatal, though. Sometimes they are innovations. The swallowtail butterflies, a large family with representatives from the equator to the Arctic Circle, evolved in the tropics as specialists on various species in the pipevine family. Alkaloids make pipevines distasteful or even poisonous to most insects and mammals, but swallowtail butterflies evolved a mechanism for sequestering the toxin—essentially storing it out of harm's way. Spreading from their center of origin, swallowtails eventually came to regions where no pipevines grew. Acceptable substitutes did, however: certain plants in the magnolia and laurel families that contained identical alkaloids. Their highly developed sense of taste enabled female swallowtails to single out the appropriate substitutes. Presented with hosts that were taxonomically different yet chemically similar, the caterpillars thrived. And, in adapting to strange food plants, swallowtails diversified: new species, specialists on the magnolia and laurel families, evolved. Continued emigration took some swallowtails beyond the range of these accustomed hosts but not out of the range of palatable alkaloids. Once again the butterflies adapted to new plants, this time to the citrus family —neotropical relatives of grapefruit, lemon, and orange that contained essential oils as well as alkaloids. Certain swallowtails thus acquired a taste for essential oils, and these species, moving northward, were able to feed on particular plants in the carrot family that contained similar essential oils. The evolutionary result was, of course, more species of swallowtail butterflies.

What we have here is a pattern of speciation based upon chemically related plant families—evolution by the sense of taste. It's less like a dance or a boxing match than a complicated tinker toy erected without regard to symmetry or balance, teetering upon its base yet miraculously remaining erect.

Like that tired pipevine swallowtail who finally oviposited on a smilax leaf, I tend to believe the testimony of sight over that of other senses. Once, forced to make camp in the dark, I spread out my sleeping bag on an abandoned dirt road, the only spot smooth enough for sleeping. It was a hot night, so I lay on top of the bag. I fell asleep quickly enough, but an uncomfortable prickling awakened me before long. It felt like tiny ants pinching and creeping. I decided it was my imagination: ants, I was certain, were active only by day. All night long the prickling continued as I lay in groggy misery, unable to believe the testimony of my skin until daylight arrived. Then vision proved what touch had not: I'd spent the night atop an active anthill.

Really, I am a sensory pauper compared to the rest of the animal kingdom. I think of myself as a visual person, yet when it comes to seeing, I can't match the hummingbird, who snatches gnats out of apparently empty air, or the falcon, who stoops upon small birds from a hundred feet overhead. Many sounds in the natural world escape my hearing. While I hear the male cicada's monotonous buzz, the female cicada, tuned to other frequencies, listens to a love song I can't imagine. My sense of taste is even more defective. I cannot, for example, distinguish chemicals present in trace amounts—less than one part per million—as dogs can. Even my sense of touch seems abbreviated: a cat's whiskers are a sensory device that help it locate prey in darkness; I, meanwhile, bump into doorjambs and chairs as I stumble from the bed to the bathroom at night.

Exceptions to the general rule that humans are visual creatures tend to end up as neurologic case studies, prodigies of

taste or smell like the man who, in reaction to a drug over-
dose, found himself immersed in a world of smell he never
dreamed existed. Pregnant women sometimes find their sense
of smell to be enhanced, but this man was like a dog: odor
temporarily became his primary sense. He was a medical student at the time, and when he entered his clinic, he recognized
each of his twenty patients by smell before he laid eyes upon
them. Less grotesque but still remarkable are the painters
who are exquisitely sensitive to color and the musicians who
are preternaturally attuned to sound. Do they have special
gifts denied to me, or am I too lazy to stretch my senses to
their utmost capacity? Perhaps, if we only knew how to go
about it, we could all be like the Punan Dyak tribe of Bor-
neo: without use of instruments or stars, they travel dimly lit
jungle trails to rendezvous arranged without benefit of telephone or mail. "Psychic navigation," some call it. I prefer to
think of it as heightened sensitivity to the subtlest of environmental cues. Poets, too—the best, at least—seem to have a
capacity denied (or only intermittently accessible) to the rest
of us: a heightened way of seeing, a sense of the emotional
weight and fragility of life.

My mother has arthritis now, so I am becoming more
aware of the manual strength and flexibility required even
for ordinary tasks—opening jars, unlocking clasps on coin
purses, pulling open stubborn drawers, lifting heavy pans.
Most of the time, until some such disability brings us up
short, we take our digital cleverness—part of our kinesthetic
sense—for granted. It is, in fact, one of the most characteristic of human skills. To hold a pen between thumb and index
finger, to thread a needle, to draw on a pair of gloves, to press
the strings of a violin, to stipple shadowed contours onto a
freshly inked drawing: these simple tasks, predicated upon
fine motor skills and an untiring sense of touch, bring us joy a

hundred times a day, though we perform them, for the most part, with total lack of awareness.

Perhaps because fine movement seems so thoroughly human, I am always surprised by the manual dexterity of insects (although I suppose I should call it pedal dexterity, since they have no hands to speak of). I have watched a paper wasp masticate a caterpillar as she turned it over and over between her forelegs like a corn cob; have seen another groom herself as meticulously as a cat; have observed a third dig a nest by flailing at grains of sand with incredible speed. I have watched a sphinx moth caterpillar excavate a burrow in damp soil: not at all hampered by the absence of hands or toes, it dug with its head, tediously shaping a hole big enough to conceal a walnut.

This hard-working caterpillar reminded me of childhood games that forbade the use of our extremities—sack races that hobbled the feet, other races that required balancing an egg on a spoon held between the teeth, no hands allowed. How awkward we were as we staggered towards the finish line with knees encumbered in burlap bags; how many eggs we broke because we could not use our hands to hold or steady. Without our normal range of motion, we were handicapped indeed. The ants that, grain by grain, build volcano-shaped nests in my driveway, the bees that cut circular bits of leaf from my lilac, the caterpillars that suspend themselves from twigs with fine strands of silk: all these show a dexterity akin to ours, yet all manage without fingers and opposable thumbs. The tasks that nature needs done she accomplishes somehow. We must not imagine that the human way is the only way.

We and every other creature represent sensory tradeoffs, ancient transactions between possibility and reality. Like the mythical mermaid who surrendered her legs in exchange for the freedom of the ocean, birds long ago exchanged hands in return for the freedom of the skies, and blind cave fish, denizens of underground rivulets and pools, found sight to be fair payment for the privilege of exploiting an unoccupied niche. Our immediate ancestors might have had sensory gifts we would ache to share: a dog's world of odor or a bee's sense of time and space. Perhaps we traded sensory acuteness for an ever-larger brain, and now our intellection keeps the world at bay.

A human born without senses would be something less than human. Never to feel the touch of another's lips on yours (and how astonishing that first kiss is after so much wondering and imagining); never to fill both hands with finished compost and inhale its sweet, woodsy fragrance; never to hear the ticking of a vespertine bat, the wistful carol of a meadowlark; never to taste a yeasty roll, a salty pretzel, a sweet cantaloupe or even mere water; never to see those lips, that compost, that meadowlark: this would be to reduce life to the barest of minima, the physiological processes of circulation, digestion, and respiration, a matter of pumps, pipes, bellows, and electricity. The life of the mind would remain, I suppose, but what would it be without furnishings?

Our senses may be paltry, but without them we hardly have assurance that we do in fact exist. They are an envelope that both connects us to and separates us from the surrounding world. Only through them can we apprehend the nature of our environment, yet they are so dull that we miss much of what that environment offers. Worlds within worlds within worlds exist beyond our reach.

Deprived beyond imagining, rich beyond measure, we fill our lives with those smells and tastes and touches and sounds and sights accessible to us. Yet this surfeit of sensation does not last. Sensory impressions are more ephemeral than mayflies. They're here—vivid, immediate, intense, unforgettable, you'd think—and then they're gone. Recent sensations crowd out older ones, and even if they didn't, early impressions would lose their piquancy before long. More than once, I have told myself, "I will always remember this," meaning the mosaic of yellow leaves and blue sky, the sting of a chilly winter day, the breath of a lover on my neck, the crackle of a bonfire under cottonwood trees; but one year, two years, a decade later, little remains except for vague mental images and these few words. That sensations so real can pass so quickly from memory is one of the immutable sorrows of human life. And yet, that anything so distant—a leaf, a cloud, a voice—can feel so real is our primary source of joy.

JUST IMAGINE THIS

The tomato vines are safe enough, but almost everything else in the garden is fair game for leaf-cutter ants. Over the course of a year, a good-sized colony can harvest a literal ton of plant material. Some of this is fallen debris; much more consists of leaves and petals that the plants were using at the time. My friend Bob has seen leaf-cutter ants defoliate entire ocotillos as often as three times a year (the slender, wandlike branches sprout a new crop of leaves after heavy rainstorms). Watching the continual parade of leaves between my pyracantha hedge and the ants' nest, I wonder if there will be any hedge left by the end of the summer. Each leaf is small enough to be propelled by a single ant, held overhead in jaws so enormous they're visible to the naked eye. These ants trim larger leaves and blossoms down to a portable size, so few plants in my garden are safe, unless, of course, they happen to be tomato vines. (The moist hairs on the leaves and stems contain a chemical arsenal that deters the ants.)

Leaf-cutter ants figure prominently in a certain Guatemalan legend. According to this myth, two young men were taken in ambush and imprisoned. If they could provide four urns of flowers by morning, they were told, they would be set at liberty—a meaningless bargain since they were closely guarded. During the night, however, the young men called upon the *zampopos*, the leaf-cutter ants, which worked until dawn and filled the urns. Watching green ribbons of leaf trickle across the ground, I'm certain that my colony could easily fill a dozen urns. Leaf-cutter ants in my garden collect the same plants year after year in the same order—fallen citrus blossoms in April, bits of blood-red pomegranate petal in May, tiny green pyracantha berries in June. These are supplemented with zinnia petals from the compost pile and whatever else is available as long as it is abundant. Early in the morning, when it's cool, the ants work slowly. As the day warms up, they move faster and faster, like a film played at half, then double, speed. During the hottest part of the day they drop their burdens on the soil and disappear underground. Their nest, a miniature cinder cone about six inches high, is situated under the grapefruit tree. When I irrigate (and when it rains), they seal the entrance with particles of dirt, but the petals and leaves left outside become a sodden mass. Inevitably, then, I'll see the ants hard at work the next morning, spreading out their collection in a huge calico apron around the nest.

I could poison the ants, of course—Bob assures me that Diazinon is infallible—but I'd rather not. They're not at all aggressive—I can stand right beside the nest with impunity—and this is one point in their favor. Also, by aerating the soil, churning its layers and incorporating organic matter into it, they probably do as much good as harm over the long run. These are not, however, the reasons I tolerate their depredations. The real reason is that I feel a kinship of sorts. Just imagine this: leaf-cutter ants are gardeners, too.

Naturalists long believed that this kind of ant fed on the leaves and petals it assembled, not an unreasonable assumption since certain ant species do collect and eat seeds. It wasn't until 1874 that an entomologist named Thomas Belt dug up a leaf-cutter nest and was puzzled by the absence of accumulated leaves. He eventually determined that the plant material serves as a substrate for edible fungi which the ants cultivate in special underground gardens. These fungi do not occur anywhere else—they are a crop peculiar to the ants, as much as snap peas and stringless beans are to humans.

To the naked eye, the fungus garden—sometimes called a comb—looks like a pallid sponge or a chunk of white coral. If you put a piece of it under a microscope, however, you would see that it is composed of bits of plant material entwined with thousands of filaments. A well-tended comb produces tiny white granules called kohlrabi clusters, which is what the ants eat.

Keeping the comb alive and healthy is the ants' major preoccupation. Like any living organism, it requires a continual source of food—leaves and petals in this case. Certain plants are toxic to the fungus, and these are never brought into the nest. The ants thoroughly lick each plant fragment—sometimes defecate on it, too—before adding it to the garden. The licking presumably enhances the growth of the fungus and may also inhibit bacteria, yeast, and molds, which are introduced by the constant traffic into and out of the nest. Like good gardeners, the ants rigorously eradicate all "weeds" at once. If the ant colony is removed from its nest, the comb quickly succumbs to disease or alien fungi. By opening and closing various ventilation shafts, the ants maintain the fungus garden at the proper humidity and temperature, and, by pruning it regularly, they encourage vigorous growth. Their conscientiousness puts me to shame. Who is the real gardener here, I wonder?

These ants do everything a human gardener does—they plant, harvest, store, and protect their crops. They do it with greater dispatch and less belly-aching than most humans, too, yet some authorities balk at calling it agriculture. They assert that leaf-cutter ants lack intention, therefore cannot be real farmers, that the fungus "crop" simply evolved, therefore is not a true domesticate. I see more than a bit of chauvinism in this attitude. It's difficult for us to admit that we share one of our most vaunted skills—agriculture—with a mere insect.

No one knows for certain how gardening ants evolved. One likely scenario has the ancestral ants collecting seeds and other pieces of vegetation on which they fed directly. In the humid environment of the nest, fungi tended to invade these food stores. For some reason, the ants did not always attempt to eradicate the fungi—in effect, the fungi were protected organisms. At some point the ants switched from eating plant material to eating the fungus itself, then to cultivating the fungus deliberately. The fact that these fungi occur only in ant colonies suggests coevolution of the organisms involved. Ants selected fungi for their edibility and cultivability; fungi selected ants for the behaviors that assured survival—pruning and manuring and planting.

The origins of human agriculture are not so different. Again, no one knows for certain how it began. The ancestors of many of our crops probably started out as weeds. They would have volunteered in sunny spots where the soil was loose from recent disturbance, often in the vicinity of human dwellings or in other places where people foraged and worked. Some of these weedy volunteers—the ones already known to be edible or otherwise useful—were at first tolerated, then protected, and, finally, planted, much as postulated for the gardening ants.

The main difference is that for tens of thousands of years, the gardening ants have been guided solely by instinct, whereas humans eventually made a leap in understanding. And what a leap it was: first, to realize that the seeds dropped from wild plants would produce more of their kind the following year, then to imagine that human hands, by picking seed and saving it and planting it at will, could control this process ever more precisely. Once conscious cultivation began, domestication—the deliberate shaping of species to fit human needs—was only a step or two away.

Beans and grains are a good example of how domestication works. When ripe, the pods of most wild beans spring open and scatter their contents all over the landscape, making it difficult to gather the beans, but once in a while a mutant plant bears tightly sealed pods. Early agriculturists, recognizing this as a desirable characteristic, saved the seeds. The seeds were planted and grown and saved again, a process repeated many times, eventually resulting in domesticated beans with pods that remain sealed until harvest. The same thing happened with wild grasses, the seed stalks of which also shatter upon ripening. When some unknown, unsung farmer stumbled across an anomalous plant that did not shatter, she altered the course of agriculture forever by saving and planting its seeds. Wild grasses eventually became wheat, rye, and barley, cultivated grains that retain their seeds after ripening. Now humans have become so skillful at directing the course of evolution that we can produce white eggplants, square tomatoes, stringless beans, burpless cucumbers.

As we developed crops, they, in turn, developed us. Selection was double-edged, and we are not what we would have been had we not discovered the miracle of agriculture and, in discovering, created it out of nothing, out of mere possibility and chance. Before we grew our own food, we were hunter-gatherers, entirely dependent upon the largess of the natural world, especially wild plants. We moved from place to place to follow the food supply, and we ate whatever was available whenever we could find it.

With the advent of agriculture, all this changed, and we

changed with it. Before agriculture, we were generalized predators—we fed opportunistically as luck and skill allowed. After, we became obligate agriculturists, unable to feed ourselves on nature's bounty alone. At first, our homegrown diets lacked diversity. Our nutritional levels declined, and more and more of us developed osteoporosis and other nutritional diseases. But, as we became more efficient at growing our own food, who knows what developments took place in our bones and brains? Perhaps we became taller, stronger, smarter, more easily able to reason our way out of whatever problems we stumbled into.

Certainly, we became sedentary instead of nomadic, and we taught ourselves to weed, plow, and plant. Our populations became more concentrated, which put pressure on us to grow an increasingly greater proportion of our food. Sometimes we failed—agriculture is alarmingly susceptible to such catastrophes as flood, drought, and pest infestations—and this meant famine, since we had forgotten how to live off the land. Living together in greater numbers made us more susceptible to communicable diseases. Crowded living conditions also made it more difficult to get along with one another, and we may have become more aggressive and deceitful as a result.

In our hubris, we often say that we invented agriculture, forgetting to mention that agriculture also invented us. We coevolved with the plants we eat, just as much as fungi and leaf-cutter ants. To say that the corn cob—a highly specialized structure that exists nowhere in the wild—hinders the natural dispersal of its seeds is to tell only half the story. The other half is that the cob does permit seed dispersal by humans, the very creatures uniquely qualified to place each kernel where it will receive close attention and the best conditions for growth and reproduction.

We shape our food, and our food shapes us. Or so I imag-

ine, since I am prey to fantasies like the character in a Peter
De Vries novel who sometimes fancied that he was supported
on a jointed improvisation of Tinker Toys called "bones." I
imagine that when I tuck a sunflower seed into moist, dark
earth, I create an entire plant because each seed contains
everything needed—like a cake mix, all I add is water. I imagine that the development of crop plants was among the most
improbable of improbabilities. How else could it be? Out of
500,000 species of plants, only 200 have been domesticated.
This is hardly a groundswell of inevitability. In fact, it is so
chancy that people have long preferred to believe that crops
were gifts of the gods or were induced by old women buried
underground.

I imagine that the tiny bees scrambling over my sunflowers
are scraping pollen into special baskets on their hind legs. Yet,
or so it seems to me, the pollen is so abundant and the baskets
are so small that each bee inevitably carries loose pollen grains
to other sunflower heads where they fertilize the ovules. I
imagine that we owe our lives to those hardworking, single-
minded insects, since without them we would have grains to
eat, and maybe meat, but few fruits, few seeds, few podded
vegetables. If bees and flowering plants had not evolved, there
would have been no place on earth for us, no niche for a fruit-
and seed- and grain- and meat-eating animal whose most
far-reaching innovation—its complex brain and capacity for
learning—was partly the product and partly the source of
life-sustaining agriculture.

I imagine that evolution has touched every corner of my
garden: the sharply flavored chemicals that make wild mustards too bitter to eat have been bred out of the broccoli
and cabbage I grow; the tendrils on my snow peas are actually leaflets that have become modified for work other than
photosynthesis; the felty hairs on my tomato vines, the ones
that leave my fingers moist and sticky whenever I rummage

for ripe fruits, contain a chemical so noxious that no insect will touch it except the tomato hornworm, which thrives on nothing else.

As Peter De Vries noticed, the natural world is more than faintly fictitious. He could even argue that if my garden were a fiction, evolution would be its plot. The difference is that plots in novels are closed, whereas the plot of evolution is open-ended. In fiction, the climax determines what comes before. The end drives the means. In evolution, there are no goals that must be reached. Instead, assorted means work toward unknown conclusions. Who would have guessed that mild-flavored mustards would prove as tasty to cabbage loopers and flea beetles as they do to us? Who would have supposed that ants could learn to cultivate underground gardens? Who could have known that Lucy, the 3.5 million-year-old hominid found in the Ethiopian desert, would lead to me writing these words in ephemeral amber on a computer screen? Who knows what will become of my genes 3.5 million years from now? Evolution continues, and I am part of a plot which is constantly unfolding in ways I can't begin to imagine.

The Green Garden
of the Heart

ACTS OF FAITH

Too often I am seduced by the colorful seed packets at the nursery. This is, of course, their purpose. The bright photographs, big letters, and fancy names are meant to entice, and it works. I love to spin the racks, thumb the envelopes, examine them front and back, dream myself into their bright and perfect world, and once I've done that much, I seldom leave without a packet or two or three.

"This is my reward for getting the garden dug this weekend," I told the clerk as I put two dozen seed packets on the counter. Giant Musselburgh leek, Red Cored Chantenay carrot, Bibb lettuce, Green Goliath broccoli, Burpee's Red Ball beet, Fordhook Giant Swiss chard and more: a cornucopia of vegetables to brighten up my winter days.

"Count yourself lucky if you do well with seeds," the clerk sniffed as she totted up the prices.

I said something noncommittal, knowing all along that it wasn't a matter of whether I did well with seeds or not. I had been hopelessly seduced by the vision of a garden to die for.

Sometimes I think that seed companies could do even better. The back of a seed packet never provides more than a minimum of prosaic information, and reading it I'm always disappointed. I don't know what I expect to find there—the gardening wisdom of the ages, perhaps. Frankly, I think that seed packets fail to live up to the promise of their contents. This could be easily remedied, however, if seed companies would only add a few lines of philosophy or a smidgen of history to every envelope. Turn seed packets into literature, because the parallels between saving seed and saving words have much to teach us.

Why not sell a stanza of poetry with Oak Leaf lettuce or a snippet of mythology with Better Boy tomatoes? Maybe boggle our minds with statistics: how many bees it takes to pollinate a field of poppy seed, how many varieties of sweet corn there are, how many kinds of lettuce. Or provide quotes from the many writers on gardens and gardening, like George Washington's "how much more delightful to an undebauched mind is the task of making improvements on the earth than all the vain glory which can be acquired from ravaging it." There's no lack of garden proverbs to quote, too, like "lime makes a rich father and a poor son." An enterprising merchant could even invent a few new proverbs like, "A penny's worth of seed buys a pound's worth of pleasure." Or, at the risk of stating the obvious, seed companies could remind us that every packet they purvey represents the continuous fabric of human life.

Other behaviors are more tenaciously rooted in our psyches, but few are more deeply human than that of saving seed. We saved seed long before we could grow it ourselves. The act is as ancient as walking down a well-worn path to fill a vessel at a pool, as instinctive as seeking shelter from a storm. The Anasazi Indians, ancient cliff-dwellers on the Colorado Plateau, grew their crops on sandy floodplains, then stored a portion of the harvest out of harm's way, within sight of, yet high above, the fields themselves. Now, in rock shelters and caves throughout the Southwest, you sometimes stumble across clay pots packed with seed that's five hundred years old.

As long as we have been farmers and gardeners, we have done this—culled the best seeds from the crop, dried them carefully to discourage the growth of fungi and bacteria, and funneled them into jars which we capped and stored in cool, dry places. Saved seed is the promise of renewal, the assurance that life will continue into the following year. Saved seed is our future. And since all seed has limited viability and must be periodically grown out to produce more of the same, spending is an act of preservation rather than profligacy.

We are savers deep in our souls. We can't help but save— seed, photographs, quilts, string, currency, jewelry, a myriad of objects, and words, which we call literature. If we are willing to be amazed by five-hundred-year-old seed, we should be absolutely stunned by a thousand-year-old text. Yet we seldom think how unlikely it is that any ancient texts have come down to us. Out of the hundreds of plays written and produced in ancient Athens, we have a mere handful, and that only by the luckiest of chances. Texts, like any physical object, are subject to decay, loss, fire, vandalism, and indifference—and to less tangible dangers, as well. As Gary Taylor reminds us, "Shakespeare's words are disappearing before our eyes, their sound is lost already, tentatively reimagined in specialized monographs written and disputed by phonologists and linguists, but spoken by no one, not even by critics who spend their lives reading Shakespeare."

The human brain is a physical object, too, and is as vulnerable to decay and loss as any ancient text. Even so, for thousands of years before the invention of writing, human minds were durable enough to retain the 125,000-word reci-tation known as the *Iliad* and, even more impressively, the 350,000 words of the *Rig Veda*, an ancient collection of Hindu hymns. At some point, however, humans switched from the durable mind to the fragile text. In forsaking the oral tradi-tion, we risked much. Thoth, the mythical inventor of writ-ing, claimed that written words would make us wiser and more powerful in memory, but his sovereign, King Ammon, argued that reliance on texts would instead produce forget-fulness as people failed to exercise their memories. Here is one informative parallel with saving seed. When we always buy our seed in packets, we run the danger of forgetting how to save it. Once that continuity is lost, once that thread is dropped, we start to unravel the fabric that makes us human.

There are other parallels, as well. Literature must be taught if it is to carry its meaning from one generation to the next, and seeds must be planted if they are to retain the germ of life. And, just as we have our literary canon—the greats whose names we learn in school and whose works are considered worthy of immortality—so we also have our genetic canon, the catalog of plants and domestic animals considered worthy of propagation. Both are ethnocentric and egocentric, sub-ject to bias of all sorts. Only the best should be saved— it's easy enough to agree on that—but what constitutes the best and who should decide? Our choices reveal more than we might want to know about ourselves. Do we preserve the old-fashioned vegetable varieties—Jacob's Cattle beans, Country Gentleman corn, Moon and Stars watermelon— that were full of flavor but otherwise unimproved or do we allow them to die out in favor of insipid hybrids that can be shipped long distances? Do we search out the life experi-ence and literature of peoples as unlike ourselves as possible, or do we focus on the reassuringly familiar—the writings of a mostly white, mostly middle-class, mostly male establishment? Too often—with books and seeds alike—we pick malnourishment over enrichment.

And so I continue to grow much of my garden from seed—from saved seed when possible. I tuck future cantaloupes, zucchinis, snap beans, and watermelons into the brown earth with hope, but afterwards I feel sad. It's alarming to consign such tiny objects to the vast, bare surface of a freshly raked bed. I'm half afraid that I'll never see them again. The possibility of failure seems great: I haven't prepared the soil sufficiently, or the weather will turn unseasonably hot or cold. Even after the seeds germinate, I fret. It's impossible to believe that the seedlings will grow and prosper. They look so tentative and vulnerable: the zucchini seedlings with a single true leaf, a kind of crumpled fan; the watermelon seedlings with two splayed cotyledons apiece; the strawflower seedlings no larger than dots of duckweed pressed onto the soil.

I find it extremely hard to wait for seed to germinate. I can't see anything happening, for one thing, and, for another, anticipation races ahead of reality as I imagine flowers and fresh vegetables festooning my garden and my life. Barbara says that planting a seed is an act of faith. She confesses that, like me, her faith is incomplete. Several days after planting, we're apt to sneak outside and scratch at the soil to see how things are coming along. Have the seed coats cracked? Are the seeds imbibing water? Has the embryo sent out its feathery radicle and its pale but sturdy hypocotyl? In short, is the seed a living miracle, or is it a promise aborted?

When I told a friend that I'd just spent seventeen dollars on seed for my winter garden, she exclaimed, "Seventeen dollars! You're brave. I never have any luck with seeds." I hear this often, and I understand completely the trepidation that lies behind it. Seed is risky. Seed is slow. Nursery transplants seem surer, faster, better in every way. But even though nursery stock promises instant gratification, the gardener who never starts with seed is like the cook who never makes a pie crust or bakes a loaf of bread from scratch. The process is part of the product. To whatever extent we can incorporate more process in our lives, to that extent we enrich and enlarge them. Turning kitchen wastes into compost is much more satisfying than buying soil amendments in a plastic bag, and cutting up fabric scraps and reassembling them into a quilt is more meaningful than buying a synthetic blanket at the department store. Growing plants from seed is no different. Our investment is faith; our harvest is salvation.

Former Christians sometimes speak of themselves as having lost their faith. But they must retain faith in certain things, for to be without faith is to have no hope at all. Though we may not have faith in the divinity of Christ or the literal truth of the Bible, we do have faith that the sun will rise tomorrow, that others will meet our needs and desires because they love us, that eventually the wicked will be punished and the virtuous rewarded, if only by their own natures. We have faith that we will be alive tomorrow, even though we know that eventually we will die. Savers of seeds, keepers of words, we have faith that future generations will read the words that we have kept and grow the seeds that we have saved.

HOMEGROWN

I suppose in most women the creative instinct displays itself in the planning and decoration of a house. We are not great musicians—there is no female Bach or Beethoven—nor painters—there is no Velasquez in petticoats.   ESTHER MEYNELL

I once believed that the sweetest words in English were *the tide is out*—that's when the secret world of swirling seaweeds and wavering anemones is revealed to human eyes—but now I think that *vine-ripened tomatoes* comes close, maybe even surpasses them. There's nothing like that explosion of tomato flavor in the mouth, especially after the long drought of winter and spring when the only fresh tomatoes available are perfectly formed impostors so heartbreakingly anemic that you wonder if they were ever attached to a vine or whether they didn't plop out of a vending machine instead. I read in the paper recently that breeders are putting the flavor back into store-bought tomatoes: sure, I said, and they're funneling the toothpaste back into the tube, too. In the meantime, I refuse to buy tomatoes at the supermarket, and from September to May my green salads are quite literally that—green—as innocent of tomatoes as Europe before Cortez. It's a moral stance as well as a culinary one. I may have to put up with quarters filled with copper and orange juice made from concentrate, but I draw the line at aluminum baseball bats and celluloid tomatoes. Where's the authenticity in a life based upon substitutes?

My tomato season begins on New Year's Day when I plant several seeds in each of six or seven milk cartons. Every year, the temptation to plant all the seeds in the package is nearly insurmountable. In the middle of winter, the prospect of forty or fifty tomato vines seems not daunting but exhilarating, and someday, if I ever have enough garden space, I may succumb. By the end of February, the seedlings are strong enough to set in the ground, which I do, even though the danger of frost won't be over for two more weeks. I follow the weather reports, and, if cold nights threaten, I cover the plants with heavy paper bags.

An early start is important here because our climate is marginal for tomato growing. The flowers won't set fruit when temperatures are below fifty-five degrees or above one hundred, and, since March nights are generally chilly and June days are invariably hot, we have only a small window of opportunity for tomato set. When an unusually cool spring combines with an extraordinarily hot summer, this window narrows to a slit.

In my garden, fruit set usually begins by the end of March. Until then, flowers open, wait, then fall barren to the ground, a source of anxiety with June just around the corner. Gardening books sometimes suggest that you can improve fruit set by shaking the flower stalks or tapping them sharply with a pencil. Certainly this won't harm the plants, but I think the benefits are mostly psychological. If you look at a tomato flower under a hand lens, you'll see that the five anthers are arranged in a ring, creating a cylinder of empty space where pollen collects. In elongating through this mass of pollen, the pistil becomes pollinated, and, if all goes well, the fertilized ovary develops into a fruit. This is self-fertilization, a process that requires no intermediaries—no bees, no butterflies, no anxious gardeners equipped with pencils. All it takes is reasonably warm temperatures and an adequate supply of mature leaves, which provide nutrient materials. (Sugars are the foremost of these, but laboratory scientists have been able to ripen tomatoes in petri dishes by injecting the immature fruits with any number of chemical compounds, including amino acids, ascorbic acid and, rather perversely, tomato juice.)

No larger than glass pinheads at first, the fruits swell rapidly, and by the end of April they are visibly ripening, losing that raw green color and beginning to blush pale orange from the bottom up. As more and more leaves are produced, the pace of fruit set increases, and the burden of fruits pulls the branches down. The plants themselves, flourishing and undisciplined, sprawl across the ground, badly needing to be staked. Their leaves and branches are clammy to the touch, leaving an impression of dampness, but, oddly, there's never any moisture to brush away.

For tomatoes set out in late February, the moment of perfect ripeness comes some time in May—never early enough. When ripe, a tomato is bright red from top to bottom. Vermilion will not do; they must be red to be fully sweet. My six tomato vines produce only one or two ripe tomatoes at first. These are precious objects, and I prepare them simply. Later in the season, when tomatoes are abundant, I fix spaghetti sauce or cheese and tomato pie. But for now, I slice the tomatoes, drizzle them with olive oil and seasoned rice vinegar, and sprinkle fresh chopped basil, salt, and pepper on top. This is a dish to be eaten at room temperature, since chilling masks its sweetness. In a week or two, I will have enough tomatoes for gazpacho, a cold soup involving chopped tomatoes, cucumbers, and parsley in a broth of tomato and v-8 juices. A soupçon of red wine vinegar and generous dashes of salt and pepper are the only seasonings I use. Some cooks add bread crumbs and olive oil, but I prefer generous amounts of tomato as the thickener.

During June and July, the wealth of tomatoes set in May continues to ripen at a steady pace, providing ample material for more gazpacho, cheese and tomato pie, stuffed tomatoes, garden tomato sauce, bacon-lettuce-and-tomato sandwiches, tomato salads, tomato soup (which is nothing like the canned product), and on and on. The cheese and tomato pie is the best of the lot, equally delicious hot or cold and well repaying the effort required. A homemade pie crust, lightly baked, is the base. Into this I spoon three diced onions that have been sauteed in liberal amounts of butter. A layer of tomato sauce is next, and this must be homemade, too, from three pounds of tomatoes lovingly peeled and seeded then cooked with a sautéed onion, minced garlic, fresh chopped basil, and salt and pepper until quite thick, nearly thick enough to burn onto the saucepan. Finally, I hide the tomato sauce under thinly sliced mozzarella and make a decoration of sliced black olives on top before I bake the pie in a 350-degree oven for thirty minutes.

The first summer I grew tomatoes, I regarded them as treasures to be hoarded for special recipes only and parceled out judiciously to the very best of friends. Perhaps in reaction, I determined that I would have a tomato deluge the following summer. I succeeded too well. Coming back mid-June from a two-week vacation, I found ten tomatoes in the refrigerator, left there by my daughter, who had watered the garden in my absence. This seemed a reasonable harvest until I stepped out the back door and discovered that my tomato vines were collapsing under ripe fruit. Bringing tomatoes indoors a dozen at a time, it took an hour to pick them all. When I finished, the entire surface of the kitchen table was hidden by tomatoes, forty-five pounds altogether. I prided myself that, as organic tomatoes, they were worth one hundred eighty dollars at a local market. For once in my life, I had enough tomatoes to fill the big wicker laundry basket, enough to make a gallon of pizza sauce, enough to share with even casual acquaintances. Enough, too, to keep me in the kitchen for several days or more. Too late, I remembered the words of Satchel Paige, who said, "Don't look back. Something might be gaining on you." Undoubtedly he had a garden in mind.

Gardening makes homebodies of us all, and during the summer of the tomatoes I became, to my dismay, more firmly tied to my kitchen than a cat to its tail. This was the summer of the cucumbers, too, so the pressure of produce from the garden was like the surge of unruly fans at a rock concert, and I was a lone Pinkerton guard trying to hold them back. Forty-five pounds of tomatoes! How could I possibly use them all before they spoiled? I rifled my cookbooks for tomato recipes—scalloped tomatoes, baked tomatoes, pickled tomatoes, Cuban tomatoes, tomato risotto, fried green tomatoes —and, hoping that tomato cake couldn't be as bad as it sounded, discovered that it could. As I stood at the sink, slipping skins off tomatoes, then scooping out their insides, I was struck by the thought that although I refused to iron clothes, I was perfectly willing to peel and seed tomatoes. Equally amazing was the fact that I, who had never canned so much as a peach, had repaired to the hardware store where I had bought every conceivable canning accessory: jelly jars, pint jars, jar lids, a jar rack, a jar lifter, a jar wrench, and, most important of all, a huge enamel pot called a hot-water canner, a kettle so big that it wouldn't fit in any cupboard. As it turned out, this didn't matter because it was in use every day for most of the summer.

It didn't rest and neither did I. Daily I stood in the kitchen, seeding tomatoes, slicing cucumbers, chopping onions, dicing green peppers, salting them down, boiling them up, spooning them into the sterile jars that waited like baby birds, mouths gaping, to be filled. Daily the house was redolent of onion and spices, and my mind was redolent with memories of my mother and grandmother bottling peaches and pears. Daily the hot-water canner steamed on the stove top, lid rattling and jars clanking, as noisy as a freight train. Usually, all four stove burners were going simultaneously: one for the canner, another for sterilizing the lids and metal bands, a third for sterilizing jars, and a fourth for cooking the chili sauce or pickle brine. I savored the irony of the gardener's life: in winter, when canning would be a cozy operation, filling the chilly kitchen with welcome warmth, the garden produces naught, but in summer, when every extra degree of heat adds to the day's burdens, the garden overflows.

As my days became a constant round of slicing and dicing, brining and whining, I complained that there must be better things to do with my time. There were books to read, journals to fill, woodwork to paint, mountains to climb, but I could do none of it, awash as I was in a sea of tomatoes and cucumbers, going down for the third time. I told family and friends that I was "sinking into domesticity," not certain if I was joking or not, half afraid that I would sink out of sight.

That was my deepest fear: drowning in that all-too-tempting, all-too-natural, all-too-easy role. Spending my days in the kitchen and my evenings poring over cookbooks, I was catapulted backwards in time to the beginning of my first marriage twenty years before, when a really good recipe for ground beef was more precious than gold fillings and making a perfect soufflé seemed more important than achieving peace in our time. In those days I fully agreed with Esther Meynell that "women express themselves in the colour of their curtains, the placing of a table or a bowl of flowers." Scrubbing, dusting, sewing, baking, I was the perfect little wife in her perfect little life. My then father-in-law congratulated my husband on the fact that I had taken to homemaking like a duck to water. He meant it as a compliment. Even more amazing, I regarded it as one.

Sometimes I want to shake her by the shoulders, that young wife so eager to please, so devoted to her kitchen and her husband, but I should be kinder. That was all she had. Only when chopping fresh herbs, flouring a chicken breast, kneading dough, dicing onions, preparing a roux, did she feel any confidence in herself or her abilities. Only when praised for the meal on the table did she feel a sense of worth. Asked to say one positive thing about herself, it was always, "I'm a good cook."

The women's movement eventually came along and taught me to question all that—the compliments and the cooking, the perfection, and the tininess of the goals that made perfection possible. Look, it said, there are other, more interesting, lives you can lead. It suggested that, contra Meynell, perhaps there could be (or already had been!) a female Bach or Beethoven, a Velasquez in petticoats. Once stated clearly and plainly, these truths seemed self-evident. So why, I wondered now, was I spending every free moment in the kitchen? I hadn't subscribed to *Ms. Magazine* for ten years only to end up sweating over kettles of boiling water. Surely there was something more important to do than drag a hose around the yard and pack tomatoes into jars?

About that time, I found a bird's nest on the driveway. Gusty winds had evidently knocked it out of the palm tree. The nest had not been used yet—there were no droppings inside nor any broken eggs on the ground. It was bowl-shaped, about the size of a bread-and-butter plate, with an inner hollow not much wider than a teacup. The outer part was a thick swirl of green weeds—the upper stems of pepper grass, shepherd's purse, and London rocket—roughly twined together. Inside this was a thick layer of woolly plant material—probably cudweed—again, the upper stems only. Very fine grass fibers pressed flat made a soft lining, and the innermost layer of all, only partially completed, was thistledown.

Out of curiosity, I showed it to my cat. She recognized it as something more than a clump of weeds and tugged and worried the outer layer with her teeth until I took the nest away. I couldn't let her destroy it because suddenly I, too, recognized it as something more. Standing there in the driveway with a partly finished bird's nest in my hand, I understood that we are animals and the need for a home is built into our psyches.

Convinced that nothing of value could come out of the kitchen, I had for some years turned my back on all the womanly tasks I'd learned and loved as a teenager—sewing, decorating, cooking—and with what results? The need to eat didn't go away simply because I decided I didn't like to cook. The need for a place to live didn't disappear just because I wouldn't spend time making curtains and dusting knick-knacks. The problem is to achieve a balance.

I learned a lot that summer of the tomatoes. I learned that I never want to grow so many tomatoes again. I learned that I wouldn't drown in domesticity, I would float. I learned that homemaking is literally the creation of a home with all that implies about renewal and comfort and protection. And I learned that feminists need homes, too.

OF TIME AND THE GARDEN

This is one of the things that I love best: the easy, intimate communication of hand and paper, words and mind, as I scribble in a yellow spiral-bound notebook, filling page after page with the minutiae of my garden. "The first female flowers are appearing on the cucumbers now," I write in May, or "The snow peas have a few tentative pods," I announce in October.

Most of the entries are equally unmemorable. If I hadn't recorded it, I would certainly not remember that on May 21, I tied the tomato vines onto an improvised trellis. "My hands are green and pungent," I wrote and noted that I accidentally broke one branch but "mended it with duct tape in the probably futile hope that it will survive long enough to ripen its burden of fruits." No one else could possibly find any interest in when the California poppies germinated or how warm it was when the lettuce bolted, yet these and like entries fascinate me inexplicably, fascinate me in the writing of them at least, so that I keep on jotting them down.

There are practical reasons for keeping a garden journal, of course, and most gardening books spell them out: if you make a note of which varieties you plant, when you plant them, when they germinate and flower, how they taste, what pests bother them, how often you irrigate, and when you fertilize, you'll have a personalized, detailed record of what works and what doesn't. I meant for mine to be this kind of useful, sensible journal from the start, but somehow it hasn't worked out that way. When I plant snow peas in September, I don't bother to look up journals from previous years to see how long they should take to germinate. They take how long they take, and that's all there is to it. There would also be a certain value, I suppose, in knowing exactly when I pick the first tomato every year, but I don't bother to look that up either.

Instead, my garden journal has become a catchall. It's a useful place for storing quotes, for instance. "Nothing builds character in a worm like a good rototilling," says Patrick McManus. "What is a garden but a species of desire?" asks Bonnie Marranca. It's the perfect place for storing recipes, too, since, as any cook knows, it's much harder to relocate a good recipe than to stumble across one the first time. Now I'll always know where to find the directions for garden quiche—my own invention, I say, as proud as the White Knight whose bumblings used to wring my heart.

I've kept other kinds of diaries over the years, but none of them pleases me the way my garden journal does, which, telling of lives other than my own, hints at wider concerns. In its pages the goldfish cluster under a lily pad, then, two by two, dart out and return, like basketball players running drills. Hovering and inspecting, paper wasps cruise the pyracantha branches—the KGB of the insect world. A bumblebee works the Mexican sunflowers, then, with its pollen baskets bulging like tightly packed saddlebags, buzzes away. Life, death, love, sex: it's all contained in my garden journal, which brims with the comings and goings of hundreds of animals.

Merely by writing these things down, I indicate that I value them at a different rate than ordinary life. These are the special events, I imply, the out-of-the-ordinary times that I will want to remember when, immured in a tiny apartment or fingers frozen with arthritis, I can no longer garden. Instead of putting up tomatoes, peaches, and corn, I put up observations, sensations, and small epiphanies. "Funny how hard it is to actually *see* peas on the vine," I write on February 17. "It's like searching for a doily on a snowbank. Much easier to find them by feel, by the way the plump pods dangle into your hands, like unexpected fingers or fat little goldfish." After gardening for a year, I tell my journal how, when I sink my trowel into the soil, "the dirt looks like a honeycomb, so riddled is it with earthworm burrows. This is progress indeed. Last summer a stony, barren waste; this spring a moist, rich haven."

These experiences may be objectively small, but if I mine them for all they can yield, they might prove rich indeed. My garden journal is yet another way of leading a full life in a small place. This is the traditional womanly role, of course. While men have roamed the seas in tall ships, fought wars, and conquered exotic peoples, women have stayed at home, exploring themselves and their relationships, finding wide worlds of their own within the narrow boundaries of house, garden, and town. And sometimes, leafing through nine spiral-bound notebooks, I think this might not be altogether a bad thing.

I lay plans in my garden journals, plans for that Platonic garden where beauty is truth, truth beauty, and there's never a gap in flowering from March to October. "What I really want is an English cottage garden, full of color, higgledy-piggledy, tall in the middle, with paths winding through it," I write on April 16. I decide to turn the biggest bed into a flower island, a mixture of annuals and perennials that will provide color all year long. As far as vegetables are concerned, I shall concentrate on the few crops I really love, the ones the supermarket can't match. "I can do without homegrown eggplant, peppers, leeks, carrots, chard; the only reason I planted them in the first place was because it seemed like the gardenly thing to do," I confess. Certainly, I'll move the fish pond: it's too small, too shaded, and too close to the mulberry tree. On and on it goes for pages, complete with diagrams drawn to scale and lists of plants to be tried here and there. Putting my dream garden on paper, I embrace the future in Robert Grudin's sense. "In extending our being into the future," he writes, "we give new significance to present action, and in reviewing the present as future memory we help make it memorable."

My spiral-bound journals contain those unexpected insights that come when the hands are occupied—with planting bulbs, with tying up vines, with pulling weeds—and the mind roams free. "As I worked at digging and chopping," I write on September 5, "I realized once again what a refreshing change it makes from mental work. I'm not afraid of the physical labor of gardening, certainly. What I like least are the daily chores: watering, weeding, deadheading. I garden the same way I keep house—untidily and sporadically." Happier is the insight of March 21, when I use the last of the snow peas in a stir-fry. "They ended much as they began," I note, "with a mere handful of pods. The vines looked so peaked that I pulled them out today. There will be plenty of time for more snow peas next winter. That, in fact, is one of the wonderful things about gardening—its intractable seasonality."

For some reason, it seems important to record my labors in the garden journal, even though they don't change much from season to season and year to year. Every autumn finds me starting a winter garden: pulling up half-dead zinnias, turning and winnowing the compost, digging manure into the vegetable bed, preparing the sweet-pea trench. Every spring finds me spraying *Bacillus thuringiensis* on my Swiss chard, snipping spent flowers from sweet peas, and jerry-rigging trellises for cucumbers grown unexpectedly lush. Writing these activities down, I prove how productively I use my free time, and prove, too, my tacit belief that productive use of time somehow justifies my existence—makes it okay that I occupy space, consume resources, emit pollutants.

My garden journal makes me aware of how I use time, makes me wonder, even, about the oddness of that phrase, since we don't literally use it as we do a bag of manure or a packet of seed. One Wednesday, recuperating from a mild cold, I spent a lazy morning in the garden, pulling an occasional weed but mostly basking in the sunshine like a lizard, guiltily aware of how luxurious this would seem to 90 percent of the world's population. Despite being sick, I lived a day that was close to my ideal: up at five o'clock, drinking coffee until five-thirty, writing until eight, a slow walk, a light breakfast, then desultory gardening and note taking the rest of the day. How fortunate I felt not to have necessity dictate how I spent my time that day, which was more like a Saturday or Sunday than a weekday.

I thought of how humans have always defined time as sacred or profane, sacred time being devoted to religious rituals, profane time to making a living. Now the weekend, forty-eight hours devoted to ourselves, has become our sacred time. Wouldn't we be happier if we could live like the Balinese? They squeeze necessary chores and occupations into as few hours as possible so as to leave more time—sacred time—free for the enjoyment and celebration of life.

Reading my garden journal, I realize that garden time is different from clock and calendar time. When I work outside, I use time the way our ancestors used it. The Nuer of the upper Nile valley, for instance, mark time not with equinox or solstice but with the seasonal cycles of rain and drought. The advent of the rains means that it's time to settle in permanent villages and to plant crops. The return of drought signals the transition to temporary camps where they fish and hunt. Time is hardly measured in our sense: they have no 365-day year divided into twelve artificial and arbitrary months. The length of their year goes undetermined, and they look to nature to announce the change from one season to the next. In just this way, as every gardener knows, the calendar is no authority on when to plant peas or harvest corn. We pay attention instead to trends of warming days or cooling nights. As we watch for milky fluid in corn kernels, netting on cantaloupes, and fullness in pea pods, nature herself is our almanac.

My garden journal reminds me that a garden is a series of moments that somehow metamorphose into months and seasons and years. On June 18, a gentle misting rain starts at sunset. Sitting underneath the mulberry tree, I write, "Lovely gray clouds, soft and easy on the eyes, the air in the distance thick with moisture." The mulberry makes a green and leafy umbrella, and I can hardly feel the droplets. Six months later, after the first hard frost, I note that "mulberry leaves fall, one or two each second, as the first rays of sun strike them. Some somersault over and over, others drift straight down. Hundreds of leaves lie on the ground, stems pointing upward, like shoals of single-masted boats on a choppy sea." These and other predictable annual events put me in touch with time as little else can.

Reading old garden journals, I understand that the garden is a metaphor for perfect integration. Cyclical time and linear time meet and mingle at last as the garden rolls through the seasons and progresses through successive years. The opposing forces of process and goal are reconciled, too: there is no contradiction between planting a *Sequoia* seed and harvesting a bucketful of snap peas. Even success and failure, it appears, are not diametric opposites but complementary powers, like the left and right ventricles of the heart.

Without my garden journal, I might forget what I have so painfully learned. I'd be like the newly emerged sphinx moth that took off without a backward glance, intent only on the business of being an adult, its past life on leaves and in the soil as completely forgotten as if it had never happened. Or, worse yet, I'd be like Jimmy, a neurological patient who could not remember any event that was more than an hour old. He lived in a continuous present, a man without a past— almost a man without a human core, for it is the sum of all our past moments that makes us what we are in the present and predicts what we might be in the future.

My garden, my time, my life. It is my garden journal that makes me realize how closely they are connected. I started a garden journal as I started a garden—without understanding why. The need to do so came first, and in the doing of it came the understanding. This, then, is one of the things that I love best: the intimate communication of hand and paper, pen and page—a quiet voice talking to time in the easy expectation that time will eventually reply.

THE USES OF GARDENS

A garden gives interest a place, and it proves one's place interesting and worthy of interest.   WENDELL BERRY

The possibilities for gardens are limitless. There are butterfly gardens, wildflower gardens, hummingbird gardens, herb gardens, water gardens, moon gardens, fragrance gardens, rose gardens, azalea gardens, Bible gardens, Shakespeare gardens, and many more. Mine, I finally learned, is a kitchen garden, which is not to say that it doesn't provide butterflies, hummingbirds, and fragrance aplenty. "Kitchen garden" is the perfect phrase for what my garden is—a plot of ground just outside the back door where I grow a haphazard mixture of vegetables, herbs, and flowers. The use of my garden is implicit in its definition: it is meant to provide ripe tomatoes for salads and sandwiches, sweet peas to stuff into Mason jars, and cup after cup of basil leaves for mashing into pesto.

Other kinds of gardens have other uses. Some are meant as retreats, like medieval pleasure gardens. We know about these small, enclosed spaces from woodcuts, paintings, and illuminated manuscripts. "Care must be taken," a medieval gardener wrote, "that the lawn is of such a size that about it . . . may be planted every sweet-smelling herb such as rue, and sage and basil, and likewise all sorts of flowers, as the violet, columbine, lily, rose, iris, and the like. . . . Let there be a higher bench of turf flowering and lovely; and somewhere in the middle provide seats so that men may sit down there to take their repose pleasurably when their senses need refreshment."

Our gardens can be retreats, but just as often they are also places where the gardener engages the outside world in a continuing conversation. Gardeners skilled at growing wildflowers, for example, sometimes volunteer to help preserve endangered plants. They propagate rare species so that the plants can be established in likely habitats in the wild. In Great Britain, suburban gardens are having a salutary impact on populations of rare butterflies. By growing the proper host plants, gardeners keep rare butterflies alive and prevent further inroads on dwindling butterfly diversity. Seed savers who grow heirloom varieties like Jacob's Cattle beans and Moon and Stars watermelon are preserving diversity, too. Their gardens are reservoirs for the genetic diversity that has been largely bred out of modern hybrid lines. No matter what their speciality, all these gardeners are alike in one way: they cultivate what Erica Jong calls the green garden of the heart.

I step into the garden—my kitchen garden, as I think of it now—to pick some basil for a tomato salad. Ninety minutes later I come back inside with two cucumbers, four tomatoes, six zucchini, and itching arms, having liberated the watermelon vines from the clutches of the cucumbers and vice versa. I forgot the basil entirely, of course, but that's what happens when you putter. One thing leads to another, and if, snipping zinnias for a bouquet, I'm distracted by rioting weeds, that's all right because I'll get back to the zinnias eventually.

Deep in my heart, I suspect that puttering is an ignoble

activity, yet in the garden, it is inordinately satisfying none-theless. Pinching snow peas off the vine with thumb and fore-finger, popping the bulging ones into my mouth; snipping poppies and getting dusted with yellow pollen; sifting fine earth onto the row of sunflower seeds, rocklike in their tiny trench—doing all this I am conscious only of the task itself and my pleasure in it. If I could bottle that feeling, it would glimmer in the dark like fireflies. Puttering is the antithesis of the concentrated attention required to create a work of art, but, oddly, it has the same power to make me forget every-thing but the task at hand so that an hour passes like a minute or two.

Something similar happens when I dig, especially if the soil is soft and my shovel is sharp. Digging by hand, I get to know my garden from end to end and side to side. Paus-ing to crumble a clod of dirt, letting the soil dribble through my fingers like soft, brown ball bearings, I learn the feel of loam and clay. I discover which side of the garden is richest, which drains least well. I make an informal inventory of the soil fauna, too: squiggling earthworms tied into knots, cicada nymphs waving feeble legs, mysterious webby cocoons, inert caterpillars disturbed while pupating. Every shovel of earth holds the promise of an archaeological expedition: the handle of a coffee cup, spark plugs, shards of unpainted Indian pot-tery, and the inevitable rusty nails, or, rather, the idea of nails, since nothing remains but streaks of rust in naillike shapes.

Digging by hand can't be hurried. Its natural rhythm forces me to slow down. I work at the pace of the job itself instead of at my own normally hectic level. No matter how frenzied I feel when I start, I am always calmer by the time I stop. My body may be tired by then, but my mind feels rejuvenated, as it always does when time has no existence. Carol Flinders, who calls this "working with one-pointed attention," says that during these moments of deep concentration, "we are lifted clear *out* of time, and for a few minutes the stress of the day slips away."

Robert Louis Stevenson knew all about this phenomenon. He told of a mythical village where no one had a clock or a calender and where every inhabitant possessed armfuls of spare hours. They had discovered that "not to keep hours for a lifetime," as Stevenson wrote, "is to live forever." And this is another use of gardens. To enter the garden world is to stop time for an hour or a day, for however long your attention is completely absorbed by the ordinary tasks of digging, seeding, planting, weeding.

Some gardens, of course, are not meant for puttering in, and, since the definition of a garden is hardly distinguishable from its uses, I wonder at times if they are gardens at all. I'm familiar with this kind of garden mostly from bookstore shelves. Opening one of the big, glossy volumes at random, I survey acres of ground at a single sweep—an expanse of unmottled green so smooth that the word *lawn* seems hardly sufficient to describe it. Here and there are clumps of shrubbery and marble statuary. In the distance, there might be a Grecian temple; in the foreground there's often an Olympic-sized fish pond. It's not a garden, it's a landscape, and the only puttering done here is carried out as discreetly as possible by battalions of gardeners and gardener's assistants.

These man-made landscapes saw their heyday in England during the first half of the eighteenth century. In those days, gardening was a moral act, and gardens were philosophy made visible. Common nature—that untouched by human hands—seemed unworthy of the Creator, somehow; it was too disorderly, too unplanned, too prosaic. Fortunately, the landscape garden, when designed with care and reverence, could correct nature's flaws by representing the world as God had originally created it. The great garden designers like

Humphrey Repton and Capability Brown did not hesitate to remake the natural landscape entirely, in fact. They established forests, redirected streams, even erased certain knolls and built others, all to exhibit nature at its finest.

In Japan, too, the garden is meant to transcend mere nature, to correct its excesses and idealize its strengths. As one Japanese garden designer wrote, "We love the beauty of nature, to be sure, but we want to go a little further. We like to regenerate that beauty by symbolizing it." For this reason, every plant, boulder and carving in a Japanese garden has meaning. The very rocks have names according to their shape: heart rock, body rock, branching rock, reclining rock. Each is used in a particular fashion to suggest cliffs, mountains, ocean bluffs. The result? Every garden is a picture far more perfect than nature herself, with her decay, death, and struggle, could ever be. These carefully planned and laboriously executed gardens are meant to be contemplated, not rambled through or, God forbid, puttered in.

In the eyes of some, gardening is no less a moral act today than it was in sixteenth-century Japan or eighteenth-century England. These gardeners think of their gardens as survival tools in case of holocaust. Eleanor Perényi writes, "Some days, I look at my garden and wonder if it will turn out to be the last ditch, if not for me then for the next inhabitants." She wonders if her notes on "weather and crops and such tricks of the trade" might not be valuable some day, an essential link to life during some unspecified apocalypse. Stu Campbell believes that only some of us will make it through the coming "crunch," the new Dark Age when social, political, and economic systems will break down. Those who do survive, he writes, "will be those who have become less dependent on our complete economic system as it now exists": those skilled in masonry, carpentry, elementary mechanics, and, of course, gardening. Perényi's and Campbell's gardens, too, just as much as the vast, manipulated landscapes of England or the miniature ones of Japan, are philosophy made visible.

Perhaps gardening is always a moral act, and every garden, even if it's only a patch of beans, bespeaks the gardener's philosophy. One of the most famous gardens of all times must be Henry David Thoreau's bean patch, seven miles of beans planted in long, green rows. "I came to love my rows, my beans, though so many more than I wanted," he wrote. "They attached me to the earth, and so I got strength like Antaeus." His enemies were caterpillars, cool days, and woodchucks, which devoured a good quarter-acre of beans; his assistants were rain, dew, and what little fertility remained in the soil after generations of farming. He hoed weeds every day from seven until noon, harvested many more beans than he could eat himself, and concluded that "these beans have results which are not harvested by me." By the end of the summer he had reconciled his quarrel with the woodchucks; they had as much right to his beans as he did, he decided. The true husbandman relinquishes "all claim to the produce of his fields," he wrote, an unusual sentiment for a gardener but a congenial philosophy for one Henry David Thoreau.

I state my garden philosophy as boldly as Thoreau: our gardens should embody our desire to live as though the environment mattered. Wendell Berry, who writes passionately about modern-day agriculture, notes that our gardens "work directly against the feeling . . . that in order to be diverted or entertained or to 'make life interesting,' it is necessary to draw upon some distant resource—turn on the TV or take a trip." This feeling, he says, is the source of many of our environmental troubles.

He's right; if we really love our planet, we can't drive six hundred miles for a ten-mile hike. Instead, we need to become better acquainted with the spaces nearby. We must discover for ourselves that nature is where we find it and that more often we find it across the street than across the world. The creatures on our literal doorsteps are as complex and beautiful as those on the opposite side of the globe and just as much in need of whatever care we can give them, even if it's no more than beneficial neglect. How can we expect to care for wilderness, much less the planet, if we're incapable of caring for our own backyards?

Frightened at what we have done to our environment—cursed it with acid rain, polluted rivers, ozone destruction, global warming, species extinction, dwindling forests, depleted soils—we seek to undo what damage we can. Too late we have understood that this planet is the only world we have and that its resources are our only means of survival. The organic gardener realizes this as well as anyone. The soil in her yard, whether silty or sandy, loam or clay, is the only soil she's got, and it behooves her to take care of it. She understands that stewardship, like charity, begins at home. If she uses toxic sprays, and her cat then walks on contaminated ground, she runs the risk of making her pet ill. Stewardship must begin next door, too, because if her neighbor does not refrain from using poisons, the wandering cat still runs the same risk.

Love Canal, a subdivision in Niagara Falls, reminds us of what can happen to homes and gardens when there are no stewards. Back in the early 1970s, the residents of Love Canal noticed oddly colored liquids seeping into their basements and puddling in the schoolyards. Chemical stenches were pervasive. Spontaneous fires broke out. Eventually, part of the subdivision, that built directly next to the old Love Canal, where some 22,000 tons of toxic waste had been dumped between 1942 and 1953, was declared uninhabitable. Families were evacuated and their houses razed. Even though some dwellings were left standing, the community was destroyed.

Many couples divorced. A few people killed themselves. One man did something almost unthinkable before he moved away for good. He chopped down all the trees in what had been a beautiful garden, then poisoned his lawn.

"Poor Joe," said a neighbor afterwards. "What happened? Was it a nervous breakdown, or what?"

Not necessarily. Maybe it was philosophy made visible, a terrible, magniloquent gesture—to poison the ground that had poisoned his life.

Because of good stewardship, certain Native American tribes are still farming the land their great-grandparents cultivated. Their soil is still fertile, and their heirloom varieties are still intact. Gary Nabhan, who has closely examined the farms, fields, and gardens of native peoples throughout the western United States and northern Mexico, says that these cultures—the ones that have endured without crumbling—embody enduring values. "They manage local resources in a way that is informed by what ethnographer Eugene Anderson calls 'an ecology of the heart.'" Nabhan adds, "If we are to have any quality in our home environment, in our food, and in our farming, we must seek to embody enduring values as well."

But whose values? That's the question. The problem is that many Americans, myself among them, feel no sense of connection to any past culture. Little history has come down from either my mother's or my father's families. I possess some old photographs, a few books, some pieces of china, a hand-hooked rug, a quilt. No diaries, no letters, not even a household ledger. This is typical, I believe. We rootless millions have no folk tradition to follow, hardly any family tradition. In this sense we are born anew each instant, like poor Jimmy, the man whose memory included no more than the past sixty minutes.

Perhaps this is one reason many of us garden—to create our

own tradition by stepping into the flow of a larger one. We root ourselves in our gardens. In nurturing seeds and plants, we embody enduring values. We bring to life that fruitful connection between humans and plants, the umbilical cord that makes the wheat stalk as dependent on us as we are on it.

Japanese gardens symbolize this interconnectedness as well as any. Probably, they always have. Four hundred years ago, after the great tea master Rikyu completed a new garden, he gave a housewarming party. The guests were startled to discover that the garden did not, as they had expected, open onto the spectacular view of the coastline below and the ocean beyond; instead, the view was blocked by evergreens. But, as each man bent to rinse his hands in a stone basin, he saw the ocean through a gap in the shrubbery. Unexpectedly, he understood the connection between the water cupped in his hands and the shimmering sea beyond. He realized, too, that his hunched-over position symbolized his own position in the universe: stooped and therefore humble. In this way, the story goes, Rikyu brought each of his guests into a correct relationship with the infinite.

And that, in the end, is the use of every garden, great or small—to bring its inhabitants into proper relation with the infinite.

NOTES

STOLEN WATER

10   Donald N. Wilbur, *Persian Gardens and Pavilions* (Rutland, VT: Charles E. Tuttle, 1962), makes this observation about water and gardens.

16   These descriptions of Persian gardens and *qanats* also come from Wilbur. Here and throughout this essay, I have relied on Charles Bowden's lyrical and factual *Killing the Hidden Waters* (Austin: University of Texas Press, 1977) for insights into Tohono O'odham water use.

17   I have taken these facts on local water use and recharge from two sources: C. A. Everett, "Arid/Environmental Water Use Alternatives to Conventional Urban Parkland," Master's thesis, University of Arizona, 1982; and S. J. Keith, "Stream Channel Recharge in the Tucson Basin and Its Implications for Groundwater Management," Master's thesis, University of Arizona, 1981. Bowden's *Killing the Hidden Waters* provides an excellent and poignant summary of the groundwater crisis in the American Southwest.

18   Research by D. A. Cleveland, T. A. Orum, and N. Ferguson, described in "Economic Value of Home Vegetable Gardens in an Urban Desert Environment" (*HortScience* 20:694–96) 1985,

suggests that Margaret was unlucky. As the authors point out, even in the arid Southwest, gardens can provide substantial savings over grocery-store prices.

20 Bowden, in *Killing the Hidden Waters*, contrasts the Tohono O'odham and Anglo societies of abundance.

THE GARDENER'S SHADOW

22 This old Chinese proverb is quoted in *The Healthy Garden Handbook* (New York: Simon & Schuster, 1989), assembled by the editors of *Mother Earth News*.

25 E. P. Odum, *Ecology and Our Endangered Life-Support Systems* (Sunderland, MA: Sinauer Associates, 1989), gives an authoritative and readable explanation of how the natural environment helps maintain a healthy planet.

26 J. P. Reganold, R. I. Papendick, and J. F. Parr discuss the role of healthy soil in "Sustainable Agriculture" (*Scientific American* 262:112–15, 118–20) 1990, as do John Jeavons in *How to Grow More Vegetables* (Berkeley, CA: Ten Speed Press, 1974) and Jane Nyhuis in *Desert Harvest: A Guide to Vegetable Gardening in Arid Lands* (Tucson, AZ: Meals for Millions/Freedom from Hunger Foundation, 1982). Whenever I need gardening advice, inspiration, or instruction, the Jeavons and Nyhuis books are where I turn first. George Brookbank's *Desert Gardening: Fruits and Vegetables* (Tucson, AZ: Fisher Books, 1988), another authoritative and useful source, tends to stress chemical over biological controls.

   Bacillus thuringiensis can be purchased in liquid or powdered form. When sprayed on infested plants, it will be ingested by caterpillars with fatal results but will not harm adult pollinators like bees and butterflies, nor is it injurious to humans. There is abundant information on *Bacillus thuringiensis* in a recent paper by Bart Lambert and Marnix Peferoen, "Insecticidal Promise of *Bacillus thuringiensis*," (*BioScience* 42:112–22) 1992.

27 There is a large and growing body of information on pesticide resistance. I have relied in particular on James Mallet, "The Evolution of Insecticide Resistance: Have the Insects

Won?" (*Trends in Ecology and Evolution* 4:336–40) 1989. According to Lambert and Peferoen, "Insecticidal Promise," certain insect populations are even developing resistance to *Bacillus thuringiensis*.

28   These data on aphid consumption by ladybugs and lacewings come from F. E. Lutz, *A Lot of Insects: Entomology in a Suburban Garden* (New York: G. P. Putnam's, 1941). J. E. Gillaspy discusses the beneficial potential of wasps in "Management of *Polistes* Wasps for Caterpillar Predation" (*Southwestern Entomologist* 4:334–52) 1979.

29   R. Breitwisch, P. G. Merritt, and G. H. Whitesides report on the diets of young mockingbirds in "Parental Investment by the Northern Mockingbird: Male and Female Roles in Feeding Nestlings" (*Auk* 103:152–59) 1986.

29–   In volume I of *The Diary of Virginia Woolf*, A. O. Bell, ed. (New
30   York: Harcourt Brace Jovanovich, 1977), Woolf writes that she wants her diary to be "something loose knit, & yet not slovenly, so elastic that it will embrace any thing, solemn, slight or beautiful that comes into my mind." As used here, O'odham includes both the Pima and the Papago tribes. A. M. Rea describes Pima Indian farms and gardens in "The Ecology of Pima Fields" (*Environment Southwest*, no. 484, pp. 8–13) 1979. Readers interested in sympathetic and informative treatments of Native American agriculture will enjoy Gary Nabhan's *The Desert Smells Like Rain: A Naturalist in Papago Indian Country* (San Francisco: North Point Press, 1982) and his *Enduring Seeds: Native American Agriculture and Wild Plant Conservation* (San Francisco: North Point Press, 1989).

31   Ecologists who have compared pest populations in monocultures and polycultures include J. O. Tahvanainen and R. B. Root, "The Influence of Vegetational Diversity on the Population Ecology of a Specialized Herbivore, *Phyllotreta cruciferae* (Coleoptera: Chrysomelidae)" (*Oecologia* 10:321–46) 1972; and C. E. Bach, "Effects of Plant Density and Diversity on the Population Dynamics of a Specialist Herbivore, the Striped Cucumber Beetle, *Acalymma vittata* (Fab.)" (*Ecology* 61:1515–30) 1980.

31 These details about Hopi farming come from Ernest Beagle-
hole, "Notes on Hopi Economic Life" (*Yale University Publica-
tions in Anthropology* no. 15, pp. 1–88) 1937.

SWEET NOURISHMENT

34 Odum, *Ecology*, discusses nutrient cycles in a general way and
suggests further, more technical, reading.

35 S. Campbell, *Let It Rot!: The Home Gardener's Guide to Composting* (Pownal, VT: Storey Communications, 1975), explains
the art and science of composting.

37 This quote, a real period piece, comes from the 1970 edition of
Vegetable Gardening (Menlo Park, CA: Lane Books), compiled
by the editorial staffs of Sunset Books and *Sunset Magazine*.

40 J. B. Harborne, *Introduction to Ecological Biochemistry*, 3rd ed.
(New York: Academic Press, 1988), briefly discusses breakdown products of decaying protein.

40– The Whitman quotes come from "This Compost" in *Leaves*
41 *of Grass*. Claude Lévi-Strauss retells this Mundurucu myth in
The Raw and the Cooked (New York: Harper and Row, 1969).

GREAT EXPECTATIONS

46 H. Mitchell writes about gardening and natural disasters in
The Essential Earthman (Bloomington, IN: Indiana University
Press, 1981).

47 In *The Desert Smells Like Rain*, Nabhan tells how the Tohono
O'odham mesh agriculture with the seasons.

RIPENESS IS ALL

52 R. Creasy describes Algonquin planting cues in *Cooking from
the Garden: Creative Gardening and Contemporary Cuisine* (San
Francisco: Sierra Club Books, 1988). See P. A. Opler, G. W.
Frankie, and H. G. Baker, "Rainfall as a Factor in the Release,
Timing and Synchronization of Anthesis by Tropical Trees
and Shrubs" (*Journal of Biogeography* 3:231–36) 1976, for an
interesting discussion of tropical forest phenology. In "Accuracy of Duration Temperature Summing and Its Use for *Prunus*

serrulata," (*Ecology* 44:149–51) 1963, A. A. Lindsey describes the connection between cherry blossoming and air temperature.

56 E. G. Bollard discusses ripening of watermelon in "The Physiology and Nutrition of Developing Fruits" *in* p. 387–425, A. C. Hulme, ed., *The Biochemistry of Fruits and Their Products*, vol. 1 (New York: Academic Press, 1970). Another excellent review is A. G. Stephenson's "Flower and Fruit Abortion: Proximate Causes and Ultimate Functions" (*Annual Review of Ecology and Systematics* 12:253–79) 1981.

57 For this infallible clue to ripeness in watermelons, I am indebted to *Desert Gardening.*

A FULL LIFE IN A SMALL PLACE

64 The reference to Erica Jong comes from her poem "Ordinary Miracles" in the book of the same name (New York: New American Library, 1983), as do the section title and epigraph.

66 In *A Lot of Insects*, Lutz reports on insect diversity in his suburban backyard.

69 D. F. Owen, "Insect Diversity in an English Suburban Garden," in p. 13–29, G. W. Frankie and C. S. Koehler, eds., *Perspectives in Urban Entomology* (New York: Academic Press, 1978), discusses these food webs in greater detail.

72 Odum, *Ecology*, elaborates on the health-giving qualities of diverse, intact communities. The familiar Thoreau quote comes from "Walking." It is the motto of The Wilderness Society.

73 In his diary for October 5, 1856, Thoreau says he would rather watch cows in a pasture than travel to Europe.

THE MOCKINGBIRD'S SONG

75 K. C. Derrickson, in "Yearly and Situational Changes in the Estimate of Repertoire Size in Northern Mockingbirds (*Mimus polyglottos*)," (*Auk* 104:198–207) 1987, estimates that repertoires of male mockingbirds range from 45 to 244 songs per individual. C. A. Logan, "Reproductively Dependent

Song Cyclicity in Mated Male Mockingbirds (*Mimus polyglottos*)" (*Auk* 100:404–13) 1983, reviews the reasons mockingbirds sing: among them are establishment of territory and stimulation of the female's reproductive cycle. R. D. Howard, "The Influence of Sexual Selection and Interspecific Competition on Mockingbird Song (*Mimus polyglottos*)," (*Evolution* 28:428–38) 1974, shows that the sizes of mockingbird repertoires and territories are positively correlated.

D. R. Dickey, "The Mimetic Aspect of the Mocker's Song" (*Condor* 24:153–57) 1922, argues that calling the mockingbird's song "imitative" is anthropomorphic. L. Miller, "The Singing of the Mockingbird" (*Condor* 40:216–19) 1938, says that mockingbird imitations are, for the most part, fortuitously similar to the originals. H. A. Allard, "Vocal Mimicry of Starling and Mockingbird" (*Science* 90:370–71) 1939, finds mockingbird imitations to be nothing but an aimless and useless art. In "A Mockingbird Acquires His Song Repertory" (*Auk* 61:213–19) 1944, A. R. Laskey describes the vocal imitations of a hand-raised mockingbird.

77   The ornithologist who suffered frequent and relentless mockingbird attack was P. G. Merritt. He describes the experience in "Observer Recognition by the Northern Mockingbird" (*Journal of Field Ornithology* 55:252–53) 1984. For more on the cats of Felversham, see P. B. Churcher and J. H. Lawton, "Beware of Well-Fed Felines," (*Natural History* [July]:40–47) 1989.

80   Randall Breitwisch, P. G. Merritt, and G. H. Whitesides report on the fruit-eating phenomenon in "Why Do Northern Mockingbirds Feed Fruit to Their Nestlings?" (*Condor* 86:281–87) 1984. J. P. Hailman describes mockingbird ballets in "Hostile Dancing and Fall Territory of a Color-Banded Mockingbird" (*Condor* 62:464–68) 1960. An excellent account of mockingbird territoriality is A. R. Laskey's "Mockingbird Life History Studies" (*Auk* 52:370–81) 1935.

83   L. Thomas, in *The Medusa and the Snail: More Notes of a Biology Watcher* (New York: Viking Press, 1979), notes that evolution hinges upon the capacity of DNA to err.

TRANSFORMATIONS

84– Here and throughout this essay, I am indebted to several
85   sources for information on the life histories of Lepidoptera,
     particularly M. M. Douglas, *The Lives of Butterflies* (Ann Ar-
     bor: University of Michigan Press, 1986); and J. A. Scott, *The
     Butterflies of North America: A Natural History and Field Guide*
     (Stanford, CA: Stanford University Press, 1986). G. A. Jones
     and R. T. Thurston report on the eating habits of tobacco
     hornworms in "Leaf Consumption and Development of To-
     bacco Hornworm Larvae" (*Journal of Economic Entomology* 63:
     1938–1941) 1970.

88   D. A. West and W. N. Hazel describe the prepupal wander-
     ings of pipevine swallowtails in "Natural Pupation Sites of
     Swallowtail Butterflies (Lepidoptera: Papilioninae): *Papilio
     polyxenes* Fabr., *P. glaucus* L. and *Battus philenor* (L.)," (*Ecologi-
     cal Entomology* 4:387–92) 1979. These are the same inventive
     entomologists who tracked caterpillars to their pupation sites
     in the woods.

89   Recent reports on color dimorphism in swallowtail chrysali
     include W. N. Hazel and D. A. West, "Environmental Con-
     trol of Pupal Color in Swallowtail Butterflies (Lepidoptera:
     Papilioninae): *Battus philenor* (L.) and *Papilio polyxenes* Fabr."
     (*Ecological Entomology* 4:393–400) 1979; S. R. Sims and A. M.
     Shapiro, "Pupal Color Dimorphism in California *Battus phile-
     nor*: Pupation Sites, Environmental Control, and Diapause
     Linkage" (*Ecological Entomology* 8:95–104) 1983; and S. R. Sims
     and A. M. Shapiro, "Pupal Color Dimorphism in California
     Battus philenor (L.) (Papilionidae): Mortality Factors and Selec-
     tive Advantage" (*Journal of the Lepidopterists' Society* 37:236–43)
     1983. Douglas, in *The Lives of Butterflies*, refers to the chrysa-
     lis as a metamorphic bridge. He describes pupation and the
     function of imaginal discs in lucid detail.

90   The Colette quotes are from *Sido* and *La Naissance du Jour*,
     both excerpted in Robert Phelps's anthology of her writings,
     Earthly Paradise (New York: Farrar Straus Giroux, 1966).

92   For this discussion of butterfly evolution I have relied heavily on Scott, *The Butterflies of North America*.

93   Douglas, *The Lives of Butterflies*, emphasizes that the striking changes of metamorphosis take place within an individual whose genetic make-up does not change.

93   The Saint Augustine quote comes from his *Confessions*.

VULNERABILITIES

97   N. A. Weber, in *Gardening Ants: The Attines* (American Philosophical Society Memoir no. 92) 1972, describes the life histories of various species of leafcutter ants.

98   An excellent account of horned lizard ecology is W. C. Sherbrooke's *Horned Lizards: Unique Reptiles of Western North America* (Globe, AZ: Southwest Parks and Monuments Association, 1981).

THE EYE OF THE DRAGONFLY

104   For information on dragonfly vision, I have relied heavily on Cedric Gillott, *Entomology* (New York: Plenum Press, 1980); R. F. Chapman, *The Insects: Structure and Function*, 3rd ed. (London: Hodder and Stoughton, 1982); and R. R. Askey, *The Dragonflies of Europe* (Colchester, England: Harley Books, 1988).

107   I've taken this point about plant and insect numbers from Harborne's *Ecological Biochemistry*. P. R. Ehrlich and P. H. Raven recognized early on that the diversity of plants augments the diversity of insects and vice versa in "Butterflies and Plants: A Study in Coevolution," (*Evolution* 18:586–608) 1964. Paul Feeny has studied chemical warfare in the cabbage family: see "Defensive Ecology of the Cruciferae" (*Annals of the Missouri Botanical Garden* 64:221–34) 1977, for example.

109   M. D. Rausher has made an extensive study of pipevine swallowtails and pipevines. Of particular relevance here is "Search Image for Leaf Shape in a Butterfly" (*Science* 20:1071–73) 1978. D. R. Papaj describes this hapless butterfly in "An

Oviposition 'Mistake' by *Battus philenor* L. (Papilionidae),"
(*Journal of the Lepidopterists' Society* 40:348–49) 1986. I've taken
this discussion of swallowtail evolution from Frank Slansky,
"Latitudinal Gradients in Species Diversity of the New World
Swallowtail Butterflies" (*Journal of Research on the Lepidoptera*
11:201–18) 1972.

111 O. Sacks tells about this medical student in *The Man Who
Mistook His Wife for a Hat and Other Clinical Tales* (New York:
Harper & Row, 1987). Lawrence Blair describes "psychic navi-
gation" in *Ring of Fire: Exploring the Last Remote Places of the
World* (New York: Bantam Books, 1988).

JUST IMAGINE THIS

115 This myth is retold by Weber in *Gardening Ants*. I have relied
throughout this essay on Weber's authoritative and readable
monograph.

119 In *The Origins of Agriculture: An Evolutionary Perspective* (New
York: Academic Press, 1984), David Rindos discusses the
long-held idea that planting and harvesting must be inten-
tional if they are to be termed "agriculture." He disagrees
with this notion. In the same book, Rindos suggests that ants
and their fungal food source are coevolved symbionts. J. G.
Hawkes, *The Diversity of Crop Plants* (Cambridge, MA: Har-
vard University Press, 1983), reviews recent thought on the
origins of human agriculture.

120 As Timothy Johns points out in *With Bitter Herbs They Shall
Eat It* (Tucson: University of Arizona Press, 1990), domestication was also a process in which the toxic secondary chemicals
in plants were reduced or eliminated. This happened as early
agriculturists preferentially selected the less bitter plants for
propagation.

Rindos, *The Origins of Agriculture*, emphasizes the coevolution of humans and crops. Johns, *With Bitter Herbs*, also surveys the effect of agriculture on human health and nutrition.
This discussion relies heavily on their ideas. R. D. Alexan-
der, in *The Biology of Moral Systems* (New York: Aldine de
Bruyter, 1987), suggests that living together in larger groups

selected for exploitive behaviors such as aggressiveness and deceitfulness.

121   The Peter De Vries reference is to *Let Me Count the Ways* (Boston: Little, Brown, 1965).

ACTS OF FAITH

126   In *Desert Harvest*, Nyhuis describes the surprisingly simple process of saving seed. It's important to note that not all seed is worth saving. The cherry tomatoes that volunteer in my garden are a good example. These are the offspring of hybrid plants grown the year before. Although the volunteers always grow well, the tomatoes they produce are insipid. This is often the case with volunteers from hybrids, since hybrid seed, the result of crossing between two different varieties or species, seldom runs true to type in the succeeding generations.

127   The Gary Taylor quote comes from *Reinventing Shakespeare: A Cultural History from the Restoration to the Present* (New York: Weidenfeld & Nicolson, 1989). I've taken the anecdote about Thoth and King Ammon from Wendy Doninger O'Flaherty's *Other People's Myths: The Cave of Echoes* (New York: Macmillan, 1988), who in turn took it from Plato's *Phaedrus*. Nabhan, in *Enduring Seeds*, effectively conveys the urgency and importance of maintaining genetically distinct crops peculiar to particular habitats and places.

HOMEGROWN

132   A. C. Leopold and F. I. Scott brought tomato embryos to maturity using tomato juice and other substances. They report on their research in "Physiological Factors in Tomato Fruit-Set" (*American Journal of Botany* 39:310–17) 1952.

136   The Esther Meynell quotes here and at the beginning of the essay come from *Sussex Cottage* (New York: Macmillan, 1937).

OF TIME AND THE GARDEN

140   The P. F. McManus quote is from *They Shoot Canoes, Don't They?* (New York: Holt, Rinehart and Winston, 1981); the Bonnie Marranca quote comes from her preface to *American*

Garden Writing: Gleanings from Garden Lives Then and Now (New York: Penguin Books, 1989).

142   R. Grudin makes this observation in *Time and the Art of Living* (New York: Ticknor and Fields, 1982).

143   In *Empires of Time: Calendars, Clocks, and Cultures* (New York: Basic Books, 1989) Anthony Aveni discusses sacred and profane time. My mention of the Nuer is based upon his more lengthy account of their seasonal regime.

145   Sacks tells about Jimmy in *The Man Who Mistook His Wife for a Hat*.

THE USES OF GARDENS

146–   This medieval gardener, Albert, Count of Bollstadt, is quoted
47   in Jeremy Harvey's *The Medieval Garden* (London: B. T. Batsford, 1981). Owen mentions the conservation efforts of British gardeners in "Insect Diversity in an English Suburban Garden."

147   This reference to Erica Jong is from her poem "Fruits and Vegetables" in the book of the same name (New York: Holt, Rinehart and Winston, 1971).

148   The Carol Flinders quote comes from her introduction to *The New Laurel's Kitchen*, by Laurel Robertson, Carol Flinders, and Brian Ruppenthal (Berkeley, CA: Ten Speed Press, 1986).

149   R. L. Stevenson wrote about release from time in "Walking Tours," recently reprinted in *The Lantern-Bearers and Other Essays*, Jeremy Treglown, ed. (New York: Farrar Straus Giroux, 1988).

149–   My source for eighteenth-century attitudes toward landscapes
50   is Christopher Hussey, *English Gardens and Landscapes, 1700–1750* (New York: Funk and Wagnalls, 1967). The quote about Japanese garden design comes from Jiro Harada, *Japanese Gardens* (Boston: Charles T. Branford, 1956). Eleanor Perényi's *Green Thoughts: A Writer in the Garden* (New York: Random House, 1981) is the source of the quote given here. The Stu Campbell quote comes from *Let It Rot*. Thoreau described his famous bean patch in *Walden*.

151 The Wendell Berry quote comes from *The Gift of Good Land* (San Francisco: North Point Press, 1981).

152 I gleaned these facts about Love Canal from a segment broadcast on October 15, 1990, on National Public Radio's "Morning Edition." Nabhan writes about enduring values in *Enduring Seeds*, the source of this quote.

154 I have borrowed this anecdote about Rikyu from Harada's *Japanese Gardens*.

ABOUT THE AUTHOR

JANICE EMILY BOWERS, a botanist by training and a naturalist by instinct, is a writer of diaries, memoirs, biographies, and essays. Her published works include *Seasons of the Wind*, *The Mountains Next Door*, and other natural history books. She lives in Tucson, Arizona, with her husband, Steve, and her cat, Katie.